VICTORIAN WIT

THOMAS BAILEY ALDRICH

His Life and Times and Contemporaries

Cordially, Charles Librizzi

by **Charles Librizzi**, historic interpreter,
Strawbery Banke Museum
Portsmouth, New Hampshire 03801

Victorian Wit: Thomas Bailey Aldrich, His Life and Times and Contemporaries

ISBN: 978-1-944393-97-7

Printed in the United States by Ingram Book Company, Lavergne, TN

Published by Piscataqua Press
32 Daniel St., Portsmouth NH 03801
www.piscataquapress.com

CAVEAT

In my many years of researching Aldrich, I have run across numerous inconsistencies. In certain following passages I have cited what I believe to be the most probable, as well as less likely variations. One of the most egregious examples of misinformation is found in "The Vault at Pfaff's" an archive of art and literature about New York City's 19th century bohemians in which Aldrich is depicted as relocating at age three from Portsmouth to New Orleans and remaining there until age 13. Unfortunately this version persists, when in fact, Aldrich and his parents were known to reside in at least two different residencies on lower Broadway for a period touching upon his fourth to ninth year. One of those addresses is listed elsewhere in this book.

Additionally, chroniclers of Aldrich's age tended to consider it for any given year what his age actually became on his birthday anniversary in the last waning weeks of that same year. Thus, Aldrich's age during events that befell him before November 11- the date of his birth – is often stated nearly a year older than he actually was at the time.

Where there are conflicts in fact and/or dates, I have noted them. Obviously further research would be in order to clear up such disputes, if they can indeed be cleared. In some instances I have improved punctuation on direct quotes to conform to today's accepted use. When there is no direct quote, I employed the feminine form of nouns, though now considered *passé*, to conform to the *de rigueur* style of Victorian times.

TABLE OF CONTENTS

I. THE ALDRICH MUSEUM AND ITS DEDICATION

Following Aldrich's death in 1907, the *Portsmouth* (NH) *Chronicle* suggested buying the local Aldrich boyhood home once owned by Thomas Darling Bailey, his maternal grandfather. The newspaper reported the house had fallen into "alien hands" and was in disrepair. It had reverted to a residence after 1895 when it ceased functioning as a hospital, until its purchase by Lilian Aldrich, his widow. The 1907-08 City Directory lists the occupants, the presumed alien Moses Moore, a mason, along with Mary McClure, a clerk and her widowed mother, Julia.

Amelia Patch, whose connection with the Aldrich Museum transcends several decades, claimed in a 1990 museum interview that five families were living in the main house at one time. As she was not born when Mrs. Aldrich acquired the house and this writer has not uncovered any supporting evidence (only Mr. Moore and the McClures were listed as occupants prior to its sale to the Aldrich widow) her recollections appear to be somewhat fanciful.

For example, she cites one such first-floor occupant a "colored woman" dubbed "Hallelujah," and goes so far as to describe the woman's physique and deportment.

According to our former curator, John Mayer, the Underwood House, built circa 1740, was also purchased by Mrs. Aldrich and destroyed where it stood across the street from the Aldrich residence. The site is now Aldrich Park; the land having been deeded to the City of Portsmouth by the museum in 1946 for use as a playground.

The boyhood residence of Mrs. Aldrich's late husband was built circa 1797 in early Federal style by William Stavers, son of the man who had built the adjacent 1766 tavern. She purchased the house at 372 Court Street next to the other side of his grandparents' home as a custodial residence. It was thought that house had been built circa 1820 by Mary Mulles (or Mullis) Rider, a childless widow, as a residence for nieces and nephews she had brought over from England. According to a dissertation by John Durel however, a deed transfer to Mrs. Rider from a James Day was not effected until January 29, 1829.

According to the City Directory, John Howell lived at

372 Court Street from 1918 to 1934, in his capacity as gardener of the Aldrich grounds.

Garland and his wife, Amelia Patch, who served as custodians over more than two decades, first occupied the house in 1935, about a year after Mr. Patch's initial association with the Aldrich museum. Eventually he held the posts of curator and executive director of the Thomas Bailey Aldrich Memorial Association.

Mr. Patch died in 1973 and his widow assumed the curatorial position. The three-building complex – which includes the fireproofed brick museum Mrs. Aldrich had built – was turned over by Bailey Aldrich, the grandson, to the Strawbery Banke Museum in 1979. The 1983 City Directory lists a retired Mrs. Patch, still living in the Patch House, which she continued to occupy until the early 1990s.

Mrs. Aldrich set about prevailing upon family members to return the Bailey furniture.

On June 29, 1908, the Portsmouth Chronicle reported that Aldrich's widow "was fortunate in being able to get practically all of [the] furniture that came out of the house back in its own position." The newspaper claimed the grandfather left the bulk of his estate when he died in 1870 to his "two" surviving daughters who in turn left them to their children; Aldrich himself and his Aunt

Caroline's daughters, Mrs. Thomas Lawton of New York and Mrs. Joseph Asch of Saugatuck, Connecticut. No mention is made of the third surviving daughter, Frances (nor of her children) who in fact also inherited her share of her father's furnishings as indicated in his will probated in Rockingham County (of which Portsmouth is a part) on May 7, 1870.

"It is odd that in biographies on Aldrich, this woman is not acknowledged as one of the grandfather Bailey's daughters," wrote Amy Nightingale, in her 1984 genealogical report for Strawbery Banke.

As one who has studied the Aldrich archives since 1996, this writer ventures to speculate that Frances and/or her descendants when approached by Thomas Bailey Aldrich's widow, declined to return what portion of his grandparents' furniture they had. What other reason would there be for Mrs. Aldrich's failure to mention her or her immediate family in her memoir, "Crowding Memories"? Thus, it would appear that in claiming "practically all of the furniture" was returned, selective memory is in play here.

Additionally, it should be noted that much of the glassware and ceramics came from Aldrich's Boston home in Beacon Hill. It seems unlikely that all of it was inherited from his mother's share of his grandfather's legacy.

Finally, Mrs. Aldrich was known to make purchases and accept "gifts" to supplement furnishing the house. A significant number of artifacts postdate by about a quarter-century Aldrich's departure from the Bailey household. That practice of acquisition, whether integral to the house or not, continued after her 1927 death into the 1960s under the aegis of the association. Also, according to Tara Voss of the curatorial department, Mrs. Patch eventually managed the memorial complex when a widow, and was known to have "moved things around."

Mrs. Aldrich was enamored of the Colonial Revival movement that emerged after the Civil War. Since Aldrich himself last resided in his maternal grandparents' house as a permanent resident in 1852 (albeit continuing to visit until 1870 the year of the death of his grandfather which followed his grandmother's demise by nine years) his widow's determination to create a Colonial Revival overlay in a house that is supposed to reflect Aldrich's boyhood is disingenuous.

There are those who believe the movement was a reactionary one, created - at least in part - to reinforce generational American values in view of the massive waves of migration that ensued in the latter part of the

19th century.

Whatever the motivation, credit should be given to such Colonial Revivalists for the modern preservation movement. Without them one could only speculate as to what artifacts would still exist. The movement is said to embrace any household article pre-dating 1840 notwithstanding its condition. For example, in the Aldrich Museum collection there is a drop-leaf table supported by spindles from a Windsor chair and a highboy chest cut down to one tier.

Mrs. Aldrich's most obvious revision is in the kitchen. Between 1820 and 1850 the United States Patent Office issued more than 550 patents for cook stoves alone, so it is reasonable to assume the Baileys had a cook stove before Aldrich left his grandparents' household. The kitchen as it now stands appears appropriate for an 18th century interpretation with its reflecting ovens or tin kitchens and open fireplace. An added irony is that the house itself is said not to date any earlier than 1797, more than 20 years after the Declaration of Independence from England.

Bailey Aldrich, Mrs. Aldrich's grandson, was said to have placed a deed restriction on the Aldrich Memorial Museum when he turned it over to Strawbery Banke in 1979, declaring the house must remain essentially as his grandmother fashioned it in 1908. This was refuted by Tara Voss of the museum's curatorial department who said on April 6, 2006, she knows of no binding "legal" obligation to do so.

On June 11, 1917, nine years after the restoration of her husband's boyhood home, Mrs. Aldrich acquired as her summer residence the Chase House, which was built circa 1762, and was turned over to the city by a Chase grandson gratis in 1881 for use in 1884 as an orphanage and a home for children of destitute parents until circa 1915. It stands immediately adjacent to the custodial quarters since dubbed the Patch House. Mrs. Aldrich brought James W. Hannon, her butler since 1900, up from Boston to manage her summer residence, then deeded it to him October 11, 1920. Hannon, born in 1876 in Massachusetts, was married to the former Mary E. Mulcahey and had three children.

According to Amelia Patch, although not associated with the Aldrich museum until the 1930s, she claimed the widow would arrive from Boston "and stay for the three months with her cook and her coachman and her span of horses."

In 1928 the year following Lilian Aldrich's death, Hannon was listed in the City Directory as curator of the Thomas Bailey Aldrich Museum. At the same time, he and his wife Mary operated an antique shop out of what he termed "The Old Chase House" in a July, 1929 quarter-page display ad in Antiques magazine. In the advertisement he noted the property was "formerly the home of Mrs. Thomas Bailey Aldrich." Apparently even two years after her death, Hannon felt her name held enough cachet to attract a desirable clientele.

"Now open to collectors for the exhibition and sale of American and English antique furniture and decorations," read the body of his advertisement. Hannon continued to maintain that residence until 1943 when the City Directory listed a new occupant, Clement V. Lowell.

The Thomas Bailey Aldrich Memorial Association founding fund of $10,000 was raised by popular subscription. Philanthropist Andrew Carnegie, listed in the Aldrich Family address book, donated $1,000.

More than 1,000 people were at the Portsmouth Theatre[1] (the current Music Hall) in tribute at the

---

[1] Although it opened in 1878 as the Music Hall, which is what it is known as at present, from 1903 to 1916 it was called the Portsmouth Theatre. Therefore, since the memorial celebration for Thomas Bailey Aldrich took place in 1908 in that building, for accuracy's sake it should be called the Portsmouth Theatre. This

memorial service on June 30, 1908, coinciding with the dedication of the Thomas Bailey Aldrich Memorial Museum.

At the service, there were 173 poems and 56 pieces of prose rendered. One of Aldrich's poems titled "Piscataqua River," which courses just yards away from his boyhood home, was printed in the official program and included this excerpt:

O River! Flowing to the main
Through woods, and field of corn,
Hear thou my longing and my pain
This sunny birthday morn;
And take this song which sorrow shapes
To music like thine own,
And sing it to the cliffs and capes
And crags where I am known!

According to Albert Bigelow Paine, a biographer of Mark Twain (née Samuel Clemens), a fellow traveler to the dedication wrote:

"We were obliged to take a rather poor train from

---

was confirmed by the Music Hall itself as well as the Portsmouth Public Library on February 9, 2001

South Norwalk [Connecticut] and Clemens [Mark Twain] was silent and gloomy most of the way to Boston.

"Once there, however, lodged in a cool and comfortable hotel, matters improved. He had brought along for the reading the old copy of Sir Thomas Malory's 'Arthur Tales,' and after dinner he took off his clothes and climbed into bed and sat up and read aloud.

"We went on a special train to Portsmouth next morning through the summer heat, and assembled, with those who were to speak in the back portion of the opera-house [theatre] behind the scenes. Clemens was genial and good-natured with all the discomfort of it; and he liked to fancy, with [William Dean] Howells, who had come over from Kittery Point, Maine how Aldrich must be amused at the whole circumstance if he could see them punishing themselves to do honor to his memory. Governor Charles M. Floyd of New Hampshire was among the attendees.

"Clemens was last on the program. The others had all said handsome, serious things and Clemens had mentally prepared something of the sort; but when he rose to speak, a sudden reaction must have set in, for his address would have delighted Aldrich; full of most charming humor, delicate, refreshing and spontaneous."

William Dean Howells, Aldrich's immediate

predecessor as editor of The Atlantic Monthly, told Twain while the pair was seated on a short willow sofa during the memorial service in Portsmouth on June 30, 1908, that the proceedings reminded him of a minstrel show.

Twain's own account of the dedication:

"The day proved a terribly hot one; each [railroad] car was like an oven and the guests mopped their brows and purchased palm-leaf fans."

The special cars carried the literary guests to the dedication. To their astonishment, they were made to pay for their own tickets. It seems that Mrs. Aldrich had arranged for the railroad cars but neglected to tell them she was not footing the bill.

"These people were so ashamed, so humiliated," wrote Twain in "Mark Twain in Eruption," published posthumously. "There were 60 guests, 10 or 15 from New York, the rest from Boston or thereabouts, and the entire transportation bill could have been covered by $150.00, yet that opulent and stingy woman [Mrs. Aldrich] was graceless enough to let that much-sacrificing company of unwealthy literary people pay the bill out of their own pockets."

Twain himself had insisted on paying his own way

before he realized he would have had to anyway. Persuaded by his family to do so, he wore black in deference to the seriousness of the ceremony, although by this time in his life he usually wore an off-white "ice cream" suit.

He said Mrs. Aldrich's motorcar, "a sumptuous and costly one," arrived at the Portsmouth train station to chauffeur Massachusetts Governor Curtis Guild, Jr. While a news photograph does show at least two other motorcars arriving at the Aldrich museum at the same time as Mrs. Aldrich's open car, apparently every other invitee had to fend for himself.

After the memorial service at the museum site and the Portsmouth Theatre the guests adjourned to the Rockingham Hotel for a luncheon.

Twain's impression of Portsmouth was dismal. He had however, agreed to serve on the museum's board of trustees, along with Howells and Edmund C. Stedman, a friend from Aldrich's early years as a Greenwich Village bohemian, all three of whom were living in New York in 1908; as well as Aldrich's son, Talbot, living in Boston and Ferris Greenslet, Aldrich's sanctioned biographer, also of Boston. Other board members included local dignitaries from the mayor on down, plus several more out-of-towners whose names have become more or less obscure with time.

"A memorial museum of George Washington relics could not excite any considerable interest if it were located in that decayed town and the devotee had to get to it over the Boston and Maine," Twain said regarding the train service to Portsmouth.

The first season (June 30-September 26, 1908) the museum attracted variable estimates, the highest being 4,000 visitors. The last season prior to its being turned over to Strawbery Banke in 1979, only 300 visitors were drawn to that historic residence.

In 1941 the booklet "Nutter House Recipes" was printed by the Courier-Gazette Press of Rockland, Maine. Presumably made available in the Aldrich Museum's souvenir shop (originally the pantry), it contains a forward that is a combination of fantasy and reality. Nutter House and Grandfather Nutter are from the fictional "The Story of a Bad Boy." In reality the house was the Bailey House and his maternal grandfather was born Thomas Darling Bailey, February 7, 1785 to Jonathan (an innkeeper) and Sarah Bailey of Greenland, New Hampshire. Nutter was the maiden name of Aldrich's maternal grandmother. His maternal grandfather had three brothers and two sisters: Daniel, born December 30, 1791; Mary, born February 27, 1795;

Nathanial, born June 8, 1798; Sarah, born July 24, 1801 and Jonathan, born July 7, 1810.

Whether the recipes themselves truly date to the period in which Aldrich either lived or frequented the house (1836-1870) is also not known. Listed as his (Tom Bailey's) favorite are Twelfth Night Cookies, which call for butter, sugar, eggs, milk, flour, salt, soda, cinnamon, lemon juice, brandy, raisins and nuts.

The booklet's forward also notes that the first time Aldrich's fiancée visited his grandfather's house was in "early spring" but the year is not mentioned. The visit, according to the narrative, afforded his mother the opportunity to provide the sort of repast to which his fiancée was accustomed, but "Aunt Abigail" (whoever she might have been in real life) was "firm that the girl might as well reconcile herself at once to the simplicity of New England living."

However a letter on file at the Houghton Library in Harvard University from Aldrich's mother to Lilian indicates her first visit to the Bailey household in Portsmouth may have taken place in the late summer of 1864. Dated August 19, 1864 it states:

"Dear Lillie, Tom is now writing you in regard to your visit here and we all want you to come right away. He is trying to devise the best and [two words indecipherable] for your getting here. I think you will have no trouble. It is a much pleasanter season for you to come now than later. We will do all we can to make it pleasant for you. Do come soon. My love to your mother and sister."

According to Mark Sammons, a former Strawbery Banke researcher, Aldrich spent part of the summer of 1865 at his maternal grandfather's house where Lilian, his fiancée, did visit him.

Mrs. Aldrich wrote that she and her husband spent the 1868 summer at his maternal grandfather's home in Portsmouth as well. He worked on what became "The Story of a Bad Boy."

According to an oral history of Mrs. Patch, compiled when she was 82 years old in October, 1990 by museum interviewers Judith Moyer and Robyn Mason, there actually was an Aunt Abigail by that name, although this is disputed by Amy Nightingale in her 1984 genealogical research.

"Abigail Bailey [was] Grandfather Nutter's sister [who] came here when [his] wife died [in 1861]. I don't know from where. She came here to go to the funeral, and [she] stayed 17 years and Aldrich said she would have stayed longer but she up and died," recounted Mrs.

Patch. Whether this is true or not is subject to conjecture especially given the fact that Mrs. Patch calls Aldrich's maternal grandfather by his fictional "Nutter" name and not his true one, "Bailey". Also, a 17-year stay in that house is highly unlikely since the grandfather died nine years after his wife, and it was sold by his heirs shortly after.

"Note: No Abigail Bailey," wrote Ms. Nightingale, six years before Mrs. Patch was interviewed for an oral history. "Thomas D. Bailey had two sisters however, Mary and Sarah. Either of them could have visited, or lived at the Court Street house during the time that Aldrich was there as a boy, supplying him with the 'character' ideas for the Aunt Abigail who appears throughout the book."

In her research Ms. Nightingale did discover that among the seven persons buried in the Thomas Darling Bailey family plot in Union Cemetery was, in fact, an Abigail Nutter, undoubtedly related to Mrs. Bailey.

"Vital statistics do not exist for this Abigail Nutter, so I can only conclude that she was either born elsewhere and moved to the Portsmouth area, or she married a Nutter and acquired the name 'Nutter' in this way," she concluded, noting that this Abigail was dead before Thomas Bailey Aldrich was even born.

The Aldrich Museum was closed during World War II, and the basement of the brick museum created by Mrs. Aldrich was converted into an air raid warden's station presumably because of its sturdy, fire-proof construction, to serve the Puddle Dock neighborhood which includes all of Strawbery Banke's 10 acres, plus two blocks east to Gate Street and two blocks west to State Street.

"I started full-time after the war when they opened up again," recalled Amelia Patch in her interview.

II. FAMILY HISTORY

Thomas Bailey Aldrich was born November 11, 1836 in Captain John Laighton's house, a once-owned property of Strawbery Banke Museum, located at 60 (also known as 61) Court Street. His Christian name not only reflects that of his mother's father, but of her only brother, who died 12 years earlier at age 15. Aldrich's horoscope on deposit in the Houghton Library at Harvard, notes the time of Aldrich's birth at approximately 6 p.m.

According to John Mayer, former curator, 1836 was a Depression year,[1] the reason Thomas Darling Bailey, Aldrich's maternal grandfather had placed his home at 40 (later 45) Court Street on the market in an advertisement dated March 12, 1836, but running at least

---

[1] Library research has uncovered no corroborative evidence. There were periods of Depression in preceding and following years, but none in 1836 per se. President Andrew Jackson did abolish the Central Federal Bank that year – a contributing factor to the Panic of 1837 - but the bank itself was still in existence when Mr. Bailey placed his house on the market.

as late as May 26, 1836. In it his grandfather offers: "nine completely furnished rooms, scullery, pantry, good cellar under whole of house, out buildings suitable for stable, chaise house, etc. [also] fruit trees, shrubbery, 'never-failing' well of good water in the garden with a pump to the same, on a 102' x 90' lot."

However, according to the late Garland W. Patch, director of the Thomas Bailey Aldrich Memorial Association, the reason Aldrich was born in the Laighton House is that Aldrich's maternal grandfather was having his own house remodeled or repaired. It is possible he did so when no sale was forthcoming. According to John Schnitzler, chief restoration carpenter, a cistern was later installed in the cellar to collect rainwater from the downspouts diverted to it[1].

The Thomas Bailey Aldrich House was originally built by William Stavers, a stagecoach owner and son of John Stavers, prosperous tavern keeper. It was said to

---

[1] Schnitzler said unlike the usual large brick variety, this cistern was relatively small and made of wood with a copper lining. He said a pump was installed in the kitchen leading directly to it and opined that the system as put together was not as efficient as it could have been. It would appear then that the well water had played out or become polluted as so many of the other wells had in the neighborhood even as early as the 18th century.

have been built in 1797 based on his inheritance and inherited land from his father, who did not die until October of that same year. The younger Stavers was said to have purchased adjoining property to complete his plan. However according to John Durel's dissertation the actual parcel upon which the Aldrich museum sits was acquired by William Stavers from Thomas Sparhawk on March 6, 1797, more than half a year prior to his father's death. William Stavers died October 14, 1811 leaving the house to his son William Cotton Stavers who died sometime after transferring it to relatives, Charles Stavers and Mary Stavers Robinson on August 19, 1822[1].

The subsequent estate inventory[2] disclosed that the second floor hall room (destined to be Thomas Bailey Aldrich's bedchamber) had been utilized as a storage room for blankets. Grandfather Bailey, a Whig, bought the house on November 12, 1832, with Daniel, one of his three brothers[3] from the then owner, Shadrach

---

[1] The last City Directory that lists his name is the 1821-23 edition.

[2] One of the Stavers' inventory fascinations is a "washing machine" dated 1814.

[3] According to Amy Nightingale writing in her 1984 Strawbery

Robinson[1]. On June 4, 1835, Daniel Bailey, who lived on Manning Street, sold his share to his brother.

"Daniel Bailey . . . was consistently visible in his brother's life, in business or family relations during this period," Amy Nightingale, a Strawbery Banke researcher wrote of the 1830-60 period of their lives.

Thomas Darling Bailey married Martha Nutter, daughter of George and Abigail Pickering Nutter. She was born in 1789 (another reference lists 1790), and died March 25, 1861. The gravestone in the Union Cemetery, immediately adjacent to the older North Cemetery, lists only her date of death at age 71. He himself was born February 7, 1787 and died May 3, 1870. It seems remarkable – if not irreverent - that on May 21, **just 18**

Banke research project, Daniel Bailey was born December 30, 1791 and not in the spring of 1792 as otherwise noted. He died in 1874 and had two wives: Olivia Cotton, born in the fall of 1797, died August 10, 1846 at age 48, and Nancy, born circa 1802, who died January 10, 1868 at age 65.

[1] One reference lists the transfer as November 12, 1823, which seems unlikely. More likely is that the last two digits were inadvertently transposed by the source. While City Directories are missing from the Portsmouth Public Library for the years 1824-26, 1828-33 and 1835-38, the ones for 1827 and 1832 list both Bailey brothers as living in other parts of town.

days later, his heirs (essentially his three surviving daughters) saw fit to sell the house and grounds to a John Stockell, a merchant.

There were several subsequent owners. From 1877 until late 1883 the house served as the Chase Home for Children, for orphans and children of destitute parents. Beginning in 1884, shortly after it ceased operation it opened as Portsmouth Hospital, the city's first "cottage"[1] hospital, a six-bed facility, remaining as such until 1895. For part of this time, the Bailey (Aldrich) house was owned by a George Bilbruck. On April 19, 1881, the Chase's own residence was turned over to the city gratis by a grandson for use as the new Chase Home for Children.

It should be noted however that there had been other hospitals on the islands known as Henzel, Shapleigh, and Pest, in the Piscataqua River, at least one of which was in operation as early as the 18th Century. The one on Shapleigh's or Shapley's Island was said to have been built in the 1780s and remained until circa 1821-22. This is a fine point, since they appear to have been specialized inoculation hospitals, such as a military facility, with one said to have been a "pest house," housing patients with

[1] This description defines a lack of residential medical staff.

contagious diseases. Also an almshouse or "poor farm" as some termed it, was built within the city itself in 1834 and said to contain a hospital of sorts.

According to Robert H. Whittaker, writing in "Land of Last Content . . . ," Portsmouth had a hospital by 1700, but he did not elaborate.

In 1862, land was purchased on Seavey's Island, which has housed the Navy Yard since 1800, for a hospital. It would seem however that some sort of hospital facility would have been functioning to serve the Navy Yard much before that time.

According to Harriet Kimball, the founder of the hospital in the Bailey house, this is what precipitated the acquisition:

"On Friday, January 18, 1884, application was made to the Relief Club for help for a poor Irish woman named Ann Dorrity, who was sick on Bow Street . . .

"She was literally homeless, friendless and penniless. She was lying [sic] in so neglected and filthy a condition that it seemed impossible to minister much to her comfort where she was. The people who housed her threatened to turn her into the street . . .

"In the middle of the night of January 20, I be-thought [sic] of the house on Court Street, vacated a month or two before, the use of which had been offered by the owners, the trustees of the Chase Home for Children to anyone who should start a hospital."

Ann Dorrity became the hospital's first patient, but unfortunately died a few weeks later.

Catherine Collins was a maid in the household of Thomas Darling Bailey. She was the inspiration for Kitty Collins, the maid in "The Story of a Bad Boy," Aldrich's most enduring work. In real life, Mrs. Collins, born in 1825, and her husband, Thomas, inherited $100 as stipulated in Thomas Darling Bailey's will. Initially Mrs. Collins lived in the Bailey house, and later moved to a nearby location to live with her husband. This may well be the same house next door that Mrs. Aldrich later purchased for the museum's custodians and subsequently known as the Patch House.

In the 1850 census, it is likely she was the 25-year-old Irish-born Catherine Killian. Presumably, Killian was her maiden name. In the 1860 census, the live-in domestic is listed as Katie Kellon, almost certainly a typographical error for Killian, unless of course the reverse is true.

Also, the 1860 census for the Bailey household lists Thomas Bailey Aldrich's mother among the occupants. One can infer that after moving to New York with her son to live with her sister and brother-in-law in 1852, she returned to her parents' household after her son struck out on his own. He however, continued to live in his aunt and uncle's house until his move to Boston in 1865.

In 1812, Thomas Darling Bailey was a joiner (carpenter). He owned shares in ships - about 20 of them over a 30-year period, including a half-interest in several schooners. One ship, the Piscataqua, in which he owned a sixteenth share during 1852-54, sailed as far as Madras, India, with a cargo of **ice** packed in sawdust and hay. He and his brother, Daniel, were also involved in groceries and lumber and he himself owned an interest in a wharf between Court and Jefferson streets in which he sold his partnership in 1835. The 1834 City Directory lists Thomas with a "ber" (lumber?) business at #5 Long Wharf with his brother, Daniel operating out of #4 Long Wharf.

In 1834, Thomas Darling Bailey, a member of the Free and Accepted Masons, was a customs inspector and the city tax assessor, the same year that Icabod Goodwin was tax assessor. (Did they hold the office jointly?) In 1850, he was in partnership in a painting and hardware store on Congress Street. In still another venture he became part owner of the Union Cemetery. In summing up, he was involved in many enterprises over the decades, including buying and selling real estate, and serving on boards of directors.

Thomas Darling Bailey left his property to his three surviving daughters. Martha Ann, the fourth daughter, who was born in 1816, died February 11, 1850 at age 34, and his only son Thomas A. died in January, 1825 at age 15. His surviving daughters were Sarah Abba, Aldrich's mother; Frances Amanda Thomas, born about 1825 and possibly within that five-year period, Caroline Frost, a redhead, whose portrait hangs in the formal parlor. To its left may be a portrait of Abigail Adams Nutter - not President Adams' wife, but Aldrich’s great-grandmother, his maternal grandmother’s mother. To date the subject has yet to be confirmed. However the portrait is known to have hung over the mantel in the drawing room of the Aldriches’ last live-in home at 59 Mt. Vernon Street, Boston. There is a photograph attesting to it in Mrs. Aldrich’s memoir, “Crowding Memories.” The woman’s costume may pre-date the sitting by a number of years, which could add to or help eliminate the confusion upon further research[1].

---

[1] On June 4, 2002, Carl Crossman, a museum overseer, examined the painting and declared it to be a copy of an original in Boston. He said the costume, an under-dress, was popular circa 1720 and that it is unlikely a Victorian woman would pose in such an earlier period costume. Therefore, as a copy, to

The 1850 census lists six residents of the Bailey household, including the maid. The family members consisted of Mr. and Mrs. Bailey, their daughter Frances and their widowed daughter Sarah and her son Thomas, whose age was listed erroneously as 15. That year he did not turn 14 until November 11 and the census was taken in late summer when he was still 13. By the 1860 census, both Frances, known affectionately as "Fanny" and Thomas Bailey Aldrich were no longer a permanent part of the household. Frances presumably had married William H. Thomas by then and Thomas Bailey Aldrich was still in New York City seeking his fortune. His mother Sarah had - sometime after her 1852 move with her son to live with her Caroline and brother-in-law Charles Frost in New York - returned to the Bailey home, perhaps to minister to her mother, who died a year after the 1860 census. It is believed that Mrs. Aldrich continued to live at the Court Street address in Portsmouth well after her mother died, perhaps even until the death of her father in 1870. She is described as entertaining her son's fiancée there in 1864 according to

---

examine paint scrapings for the purpose of dating the original work would be futile. Crossman also surmised the painting was "unfinished".

the 1941 Nutter House Recipes booklet.

Caroline was Thomas Bailey Aldrich's favorite aunt and was six-to-sixteen years older than he (a more precise age differential has not surfaced). She married Charles L. Frost, of New Orleans, Louisiana, on October 19, 1846 at the South (Unitarian) Church, Portsmouth. Aldrich, not quite 10, insisted on going on their honeymoon, because "he couldn't bear to be separated from her," and was taken!

In 1850 and 1851 he led as "Marshal Aldrich" a military marching group of boys known as the Continentals, in an Independence Day parade, escorting the floral procession, according to the Portsmouth Journal. A facsimile of a daguerreotype depicting him in an 18th century uniform is on view in the Aldrich museum. The lad appears quite self-assured if not a bit arrogant.

In an 1855 letter about those early years in Portsmouth, Aldrich described himself as "an only child, but not a spoilt one."

Although "The Story of a Bad Boy," his best known fictionalized work is based on that time spent in Portsmouth at his grandparents' home from ages 12 to 16, in reality Aldrich was a "bad" boy – in terms of mischief-making - much earlier. This was between the ages of four and nine growing up (in at least two houses) in the lower Broadway neighborhood of Manhattan. According to published recollections of Laurence Hutton, a critic, during the boy's stay in one of those houses at 941 Moore Street, the Aldrich family lived around the corner from the Hutton family on Hudson Street and they were friends. The houses were perpendicular to each other with their rear sections nearly touching.

Aldrich and Hutton, who became friends as adults, did not really know each other as children probably because of their age differences, but the latter was seven years younger, had an "Uncle John" and he and Aldrich were quite close. According to Isabel Moore, who recorded Hutton's musings, his uncle and Aldrich met for the first time nearly a half-century later following their childhood shenanigans.

Reminiscing how together they skated, ran to fires and operated a private theater "and they laughed as they wondered how they lived to tell the tale of their habitual manner of access to each other's garret rooms; which was by crawling on their hands and knees along the gutter, on the edge of the roofs, from dormer-window to dormer-window!"

When Aldrich turned six weeks old, he was moved to

what became his home (the present Aldrich Museum) for part of his boyhood. He was the only child[1] of Elias Taft Aldrich who himself was the oldest of six, born in what was then known as the Brettun's Mills section of Livermore, Maine, on November 30, 1809[2]; and Sarah Abba Bailey, born April 15, 1814, of Portsmouth. They were married February 18, 1833 in Bangor, Maine where they lived until moving to Portsmouth three years later.

Aldrich's father, a widower[3], had met his mother through business dealings with her father. At age 12 she was listed among the student body of the First Female

---

[1] Florence Agnes Nelson, a native of Livermore, Maine, and its librarian, in a letter to Mrs. Thomas Bailey Aldrich, stated that a Mrs. Treat connected to Thomas Bailey Aldrich by an unspecified marriage, claimed he had a sister, Albina, who died before age 20! This writer has yet to uncover any corroborative evidence. Aldrich himself, in a July 25, 1855 letter to his friend William Winter states unequivocally: "I have neither brother nor sister. I am an only child . . . ."

[2] Ferris Greenslet sets the year of Elias' birth as 1807, which is almost certainly in error, since genealogical records establish his father Henry as living there no earlier than 1808.

[3] The Washburn Journal," Volume IV, July 10, 1876 to August 14, 1882, edited by Ethel Wilson Gammen and published in 1974, alludes to Elias T. Aldrich's previous wife as Julia Monroe who was "so like her mother."

School in Portsmouth in its catalogue[1] dated March 1, 1827. According to an Aldrich biography by Samuel S. Duryee, Jr. she was 18 at her wedding and still given to playing with dolls.

Aldrich's paternal grandparents were Henry Aldrich, born in Uxbridge, Massachusetts, died in Long Island, New York in 1846; and Nancy Stanley Aldrich, born in Swansey, New Hampshire, died in Mobile, Alabama in 1865. The "History of Livermore," published in 1873, records Henry Aldrich came to that community in Maine in 1808, and manufactured scythe snaths (handles). The "History of Androscoggin County" states he did so from 1810 to 1825.

Writing this researcher in June of 2004, Bill Nickerson of Livermore Falls, Maine[2] stated that the

---

[1] Also listed was Jane Woods, 14-year-old English immigrant niece of Mary Rider, widow and back-street neighbor.

[2] According to W. Dennis Stires, program director of the Livermore Historical Society, who wrote this compiler in August of 2004, East Livermore broke away from Livermore in 1843 and then became known as Livermore Falls in 1930. The issue is pertinent only in that information had been published in the past that Elias T. Aldrich, Thomas' father, was born in Livermore Falls which did not exist as a separate independent entity at the time of his birth in 1809.

Henry Aldrich house was still standing on Butter Hill Road, although the original door and side lights were now part of the Livermore Main Public Library, a former schoolhouse. The ancestral Aldrich home was described as a two-story building with a portico and a rear ell.

According to a paper penned by Eloise M. Jordan on file at the Livermore Public Library, Florence Agnes Nelson, who served as Livermore's librarian for 30 years during the first half of the 20th century, told her Thomas Bailey Aldrich "used to visit here often during his boyhood."

Thomas Bailey Aldrich was the great-great-great-great-great-great grandson of Priscilla Mullins and John Alden, the cooper on the Mayflower. Ruth Alden, their daughter and John Bass, were his great-great-great-great-great-grandparents. The Bass' daughter, Hannah married Joseph Adams; his great-great-great-great-grandparents. Their son, the Rev. Joseph Adams married Elizabeth Knight Chevalier, his great-great-great-grandparents. They had a son, Benjamin who married Abigail Pickering; his great-great-grandparents. They had a daughter, Abigail, who married Capt. George Nutter, his great-grandparents. Capt. Nutter and his wife had a daughter, Martha, who was Thomas Bailey Aldrich's maternal grandmother. Martha, who died

March 25, 1861, had married Thomas Darling Bailey, who died May 3,1870.

In a July 25, 1855 letter to William Winter, who became a lifelong friend, Aldrich noted that many of his ancestors "are sleeping somewhere" near Bunker Hill.

"I come in a straight line from President Adams, and his son mentions me in his book of the Adams family. Being only three months of age when Mr. Adams put me in his book, he neglected to mention my gift of rhyme, which was very shabby in him," he asserted.

According to the Dictionary of American Biography, his ancestry on both sides was of New England colonial stock. On the father's side he was descended from George Aldrich, a tailor, who came from Derbyshire, England, on the ship "Lyon," November 6, 1631 at about age 26 with his wife Catherine (or Katherine) Seald Aldrich to the Massachusetts Bay Colony, first settling in Dorchester, then Braintree and then in 1663 in the pioneer township of Mendon, where he was considered one of the seven founding fathers. He died there in 1683. This information is contained in letters to Aldrich's son, Talbot by one of his (presumably distant) relatives, Marcus M. Aldrich, genealogist. On the mother's side, he traced his ancestry to a John Bailey, who, about 1620, was living at Grantham, in Lincolnshire, England, and on June 4, 1635, sailed from Bristol, England aboard the "Angel Gabriel" to Pennequid (now Bristol) Maine where the 240-ton vessel was wrecked in a hurricane on August 15, and some lives lost. The Aldrich lineage is as follows: George's son, Jacob; Jacob's son, David; David's son, Peter; Peter's son, Henry; Henry's son, Henry and Henry's son Elias Taft, Thomas Bailey Aldrich's father. Another of David's sons is Edward, one of whose descendants is Roger Aldrich of Sugar Hill, New Hampshire who contacted Strawbery Banke Museum September 2, 2004, about his relationship.

It's been said that the paternal side of his father's family tended toward a more nomadic life, while his mother's family tended to the traditional.

His father, Elias Taft Aldrich, imbued with that wanderlust, died on October 6, 1849 (some genealogical references state 1850, but the official estate inventory as filed in New Orleans makes it clear the year is 1849), when his son was only 12 (a month before his 13th birthday anniversary).

His wandering prompted his son to say that as a child he (Thomas Bailey Aldrich) had visited every state in the Union - which is almost certainly an exaggeration. In fact there is a void in the family's so-called travels during the son's formative years between ages 18 months (when his biographer, Ferris Greenslet maintains they left Portsmouth) and four years when he and his parents were known to have relocated to Manhattan. Charles E. Samuels in his Aldrich biography clearly states the family had settled in New York City by 1841 and continued to live there for several years.

Aldrich's father was a lumber merchant, who, in 1833, built a house in Bangor, Maine and sold it in 1834 to John Barker, Esq. From 1846 until his death in 1849, he was a merchant in New Orleans, Louisiana, and sold liquor and grocery items. He also had had a number of other business enterprises including investing in the commission business. (Attribution for this paragraph comes largely from John Mayer, former curator.)

He was also said to have been an unsuccessful banker, but this seems to have been largely attributed to Aldrich himself in writing about his father in his fictional work "The Story of a Bad Boy." In a July 25, 1855 letter to William Winter, he clearly states "my father was a merchant."

According to Sarah K. Bolton in her "Biography of American Authors," published in 1887, at the time of Aldrich's father's death of cholera on a Mississippi steamboat in Memphis, Tennessee, Thomas Darling Bailey had invested heavily in his son-in-law's ill-fated ventures. However it must be stated that the authoress quoted liberally from "The Story of a Bad Boy," failing to distinguish fact from fiction, and it may be compounding an error to assume that the senior Aldrich was ever in banking as the story relates. It is more likely his father-in-law had indeed invested in his son-in-law's unsuccessful business enterprises, since Aldrich first met his future wife after approaching Mr. Bailey on business matters. According to the "History of Livermore," published in 1873, Seth Ballou, a relative "was much in his [Elias'] employment." That book also asserts Elias T. Aldrich's death was sudden and "his friend and companion, Charles H. Pierpont, died at the same time."

In 1849 the year of Elias' death, little was known about the cause, prevention and cure of cholera. The prevailing theory was that it emerged from bad air, commonly called over the centuries as "miasma".

What is certain is that Thomas Bailey Aldrich's father died intestate - without a will – leaving a business establishment with a stock of spirits and some foodstuffs in New Orleans, Louisiana. His mother was appointed administratrix of the estate. His Uncle Charles L. Frost, husband of his mother's sister Caroline, was also present in New Orleans to help settle the affairs.

Interestingly, Daniel C. Aldrich, his father's brother, was appointed "under tutor of the minor" referring to Thomas Bailey Aldrich. Apparently, nothing of significance came of that relationship; Daniel at that time was still in his late twenties. Born in 1817, he was the fifth of six children and eight years younger than his oldest sibling Elias. He was known to be living in New Orleans as late as 1873. The other four children born to Henry and Nancy Stanley Aldrich, were Abner S., born 1811, who died in New York in 1848; Angela, who married Barzillai Latham, and was born in 1813, died in 1864; Elizabeth, who married William Cutts and died in 1844 and Nancy, who was born in 1819 and died in New York in 1843[1].

The logistics of transporting the body of Aldrich's father from Tennessee to Green-Wood Cemetery, Brooklyn, New York, is intriguing. There was no railroad line in the state of Tennessee in 1849. One might guess that he was transported by ship since Memphis is a port on the Mississippi River, for however long it might have taken. His internment took place the day after Christmas, on December 26, 1849. His widow,

---

[1] Source on sibling statistics (Elizabeth's birth date missing) is "History of Livermore."

who died 47 years later, was interred June 26, 1896. According to cemetery records their gravesites are located in Section 90, Lot 572.

Documents from the Parish of New Orleans pertaining to the estate do indicate that there was sufficient liquidity to pay all of the debts incurred by Elias Taft Aldrich, but perhaps not much more. This may explain why plans to have Thomas Bailey Aldrich, already sent to his grandparent's home in the spring of 1849 from New Orleans to prepare for Harvard, were scotched.

In 1862 Aldrich wrote an atypical story, "Out of His Head," set in his former New Orleans at the time of the cholera outbreak. Greenslet describes it as "fantastic macaberesque [sic], composed in paragraphs somewhat too short, after the French manner, and with an obvious straining at unusual rhythms." He termed it "studied impressionism."

The notary public in New Orleans parish listed $2,685.18 as part of the estate inventory of Aldrich's father, in terms of the value of wine, hard liquor, some spices and foodstuffs on hand in his business establishment. For example, nine bottles of Madeira were appraised for $2.00 total.

Additionally, it is interesting to note that among the

bills receivable were several drawn a month after his death, in November 1849 and totaled hundreds of dollars. A Charles Chandler, for example, was one of those who drew such large amounts from the business.

The total for the entire Aldrich estate inventory amounted to more than $7,292. Building property does not appear in the tabulation, suggesting that whatever premises Aldrich had occupied were rented; not owned.

There appears among the New Orleans estate inventory court documents the fact that Daniel C. Aldrich, brother of Elias T. Aldrich, was deposed and did so in behalf of an E. A. Searle, who declared he was an equal partner in E. T. Aldrich & Co., despite the fact that **there were no corporation papers to prove it**. Incredibly, the court sided with Searle! Allegedly, the partnership had been formed only a year before in the summer of 1848 in Boston.

There is also a suggestion that Mrs. Elias T. Aldrich, administratrix, attempted to obtain the power to become the sole liquidator of the estate, but her efforts were rejected by the court in recognizing Searle as an equal partner.

Several theories abound as to why Aldrich did not get to enroll at Harvard, which, according to an encyclopedia was a Unitarian stronghold in the early

1800s until 1851 when the charter was amended to remove references to control by any church.[1] The prevailing theory seems to be lack of funds on the part of his mother and her father. However it is difficult to believe that her father, Thomas Darling Bailey, lacked sufficient funds for this grandson's tuition given his diversified business enterprises, notwithstanding his apparent sizeable losses in the ill-fated ventures of the boy's father. Amy Nightingale, in her 1984 biographical sketch for Strawbery Banke noted that he and his brother Daniel went to court a number of times in the period 1830-1860.

"Most cases were charges against men who owed them money," she wrote.

With regard to family finances it is also known that Charles Frost, the Widow Aldrich's brother-in-law, was dispatched to New Orleans to try to straighten out her late husband's affairs. When Frost married her sister Caroline in October, 1846, their address was listed as

---

[1] Aldrich would later receive an honorary degree from Harvard as well as from Yale and the University of Pennsylvania. His grandson Bailey was both a Harvard undergraduate and a graduate of the Harvard Law School, and Bailey's two sons matriculated as well.

New Orleans, opening the possibility that he himself may have been born or raised in that southern city. His early life appears not to have been chronicled. There is speculation that Charles Frost henceforth held the "family's purse strings" and deigned that his nephew not go to Harvard.

There is additional speculation that Aldrich himself, although not yet 13 (for another month) declared that he would not go to Harvard as he needed to be his mother's "breadwinner".

In "The Story of a Bad Boy," he reasons that four years of college would delay his earning capacity. This latter position is bravado in this writer's opinion since he once wrote that he was looking forward to studying literature with one of the great Harvard pedagogues, Henry Wadsworth Longfellow, whose work he admired greatly. While never having matriculated, it must have been sweet compensation when in 1858, at the age of most college graduates, Aldrich was invited to read poetry at several college commencement exercises.

Aldrich attended Portsmouth Academy, the site of what became – until 2006 - the Portsmouth Public Library, under Schoolmaster Samuel De Merritt, and especially valued his training in grammar. De Merritt later wrote that no one among his pupils in all those years was more outstanding than Aldrich. Said De Merritt, in retrospect (and obviously after Aldrich had won renown): "With the hundreds of pupils who have been under my instruction, there is not one for whom I entertain a higher regard and a purer affection than Thomas Bailey Aldrich."

Aldrich used to crush flies between the pages of his speller, but whether that habit started in New York, New Orleans or Portsmouth is not known.

In 1896 he received that honorary degree from Harvard. On file at its Houghton Library are his notes prepared for the occasion. Their inference is that the decision not to matriculate was not made in 1849 the year his father died, but three years later just as he was preparing to enter its hallowed halls. It reads in part:

"In 1852 I was preparing to enter as freshman here; but fate decided I was to … achieve life through other portals. Since it was not my fortune to be one of the University's legal children, I am very proud to be a natural son."

Aldrich, his maternal grandparents, all four of their daughters and his Aunt Caroline's son, Charles (who would have been under three years of age), were baptized in the South Church on January 19, 1850. That church, still standing, was built in 1826 as Unitarian. His Aunt Caroline Augusta Bailey was married to Charles L. Frost of New Orleans, Louisiana, in that church on October 19, 1846, by the Rev. Andrew Preston Peabody. Additionally, on June 7, 1850, his mother, Sarah A. Aldrich, was "received in full communion," there.

According to Maria Silva Cosgrave, whose lecture series on Aldrich appeared in the Horn Book Magazine in 1965, Aldrich admitted that as a boy he was "not fond of reading poetry, though I feasted on prose." By chance he read Longfellow's "The Footsteps of Angels," from the "Voice of the Night," volume and from that time "I loved Longfellow, and I wrote poetry."

His mother was described by Sarah K. Bolton as "slim and fair." Aldrich, in a March 29, 1884 letter to an Atlantic Monthly contributor notes that his mother "lay dangerously ill a week ago, but she happily recovered." The Widow Aldrich lived an additional dozen years and died June 24, 1896. She is interred in Green-Wood Cemetery, Brooklyn, New York, where her husband was laid to rest nearly 47 years earlier.[1]

---

[1] Descriptions of the final resting place for Aldrich's parents were published in a memoir of Laurence Hutton, a theater critic, whose

United States First Circuit Court of Appeals Judge Bailey Aldrich, who was Talbot's son, was born in Boston on April 23, 1907 just 34 days after his illustrious grandfather died. On October 5, 2002, following a memorial service for the judge at Harvard Yard, his son David, of Brookline, Massachusetts, told this writer that his father regretted never having set eyes on his grandfather. Judge Aldrich, an only child, died September 25, 2002 at age 95. His obituary in the Boston Globe two days later described him as "a tall, thin man with a sly New England wit," whose judicial opinions were "pithy and straightforward." According to Wikipedia his personal belongings were auctioned off in 2003 for more than $650,000.

Mary Elizabeth Woodman (1841-1927), wife of Thomas Bailey Aldrich, was popularly known as Lilian for some reason. Born in Bangor, Maine, according to the 1880 United States census,[1] she was the daughter of

---

own parents were friends and neighbors of the Aldriches in New York during the 1840s.

[1] Census-taking was haphazard at best, depending upon the reliability of the interviewer and interviewee. In the 1870 census, Lilian is listed as "Lucy," born in **New York** whose parents were both born in Maine, and was identified as a "New York belle" in a 1915 publication. In the 1880 census as "Lilian"

William and Mary G. Woodman of Fryeburg, Maine, and had a sister, Martha, who married William Streter Richardson, a resident member of the New England Historic Genealogical Society. Mrs. Richardson's nickname may have been "Mattie" as that name appears in Aldrich correspondence and young Talbot, one of the twin sons makes reference to an "Aunt Mattie".

Lilian Aldrich said her husband told her of playing Indians in ambush behind every bush and tree in his maternal grandparents' yard. Or he would pretend the yard was Sherwood Forest with Robin Hood and his merry men running about. Sometimes he thought of the yard as the point where Captain Kidd buried his treasure, or the ground upon which Jeanne D'Arc rode on her steed, or the meeting place of Pocahontas and John Smith.

According to John Mayer, former curator, there was a stratified granite sidewalk at the front entrance.

---

her birthplace is Bangor, Maine with both her parents again natives of Maine. The 1900 census lists Lilian and her parents as Maine natives, but the 1910 census declares her mother to be a New Hampshire native. Her appropriate age is given in the 1870 census, but she – or another source - lops off several years in the 1910 census. By 1898 when the Aldriches submitted a passport application, Lilian's birth is declared to have occurred in 1858, or 17 years after her actual birth date!

Granite crosswalks like the one from the Aldrich House ran to the other side of the street, before streets were covered with cobblestone or macadam. The granite was said to have been transported "11 miles downriver from Durham."

Thomas Darling Bailey built a theater for the boy with sets and flats. In an introduction to "The Story of a Bad Boy," Aldrich places that theater in the barn. According to John Mayer the theater was in the stable. In creating the museum, Aldrich's widow placed a theater of sorts on the third floor of the house, where its authenticity as dating from her husband's boyhood home has come into question. A newspaper account of the museum's dedication reported Aldrich and his male friends used the maid's bedchamber in the garret (third floor) as their dressing room for their productions.

There is some evidence there was more than one stable (one of Aldrich's biographers cites: "a garden, the **stables**" and the carriage-house,) and that the carriage house was where the brick museum is now[1].

Barney Gatz, writing from London, on November 29, 1897, recalled childhood chums, in a piece subsequently

[1] The 1904 insurance map no longer depicts <u>any</u> out buildings. It precedes by three years Mrs. Aldrich's acquisition of the property.

published in two parts by the Portsmouth Journal on Christmas Day, 1897 and New Year's Day, 1898. In it he cited Aldrich as "another bright and shining star from childhood, precocious and attractive, not only for us but for our parents, at this very early period . . . active in theatrical and circus bar performances . . . owned a beautiful white pony on which he generously tendered a ride to any and all of his comrades who applied." In "The Story of a Bad Boy," the pony's name was Gypsy. Aldrich was said to charge his audience (possibly straight) "pins," while the maid paid with a clothespin.

Shortly after Aldrich died on March 19, 1907, the Portsmouth Daily Chronicle urged that his boyhood home be purchased and taken "**out of alien hands**," for use as a memorial to the Portsmouth author.

Open to the public in 1908[1] it was shuttered from 1941-1945 because of wartime conditions, and the basement of the brick museum was converted for use as an air raid warden's station.

Judge Bailey Aldrich, grandson of Thomas Bailey Aldrich, turned the museum over to the Strawbery Banke

---

[1] A relatively short season from June 30 to September 26, attracted 3,000 or possibly 4,000 visitors.

Museum on August 5, 1979. The gift included the house and its furnishings, along with the brick museum, but not the brick museum's contents. Those contents were turned over to Strawbery Banke in December, 1986, and included his grandfather's library bibelots and other acquisitions, some of dubious originality. For example there is Waterford crystal, purportedly owned by George Washington, an urn said to belong to Benjamin Franklin, Lord Byron's tea caddy and a silver cup, associated with Napoleon Bonaparte.

Married Life and Subsequent Issue

In New York, in the fall of 1862 at a party given by Edwin and Mary (Devlin) Booth, Aldrich met Mary Elizabeth (commonly known as Lilian) Woodman. They became engaged on February, 22, 1863[1] and were

[1] Among the family papers in the Houghton Library at Harvard filed under Call#6 MS AM1430 is one in which Lilian declares the engagement broken April 29, 1863. Apparently romantic brinkmanship is in play here, for within hours Aldrich's hand is forced in a note to pledge "the same depth of love that you offer me," adding: "Surely that ought to render you happy, if you are not the most unreasonable of women dear." Aldrich began the note with an intriguing comparison: "The trouble of last night is not the trouble of this morning." Unfortunately the missive containing Lilian's declaration was missing or misplaced at the

married in New York, November 28, 1865[1] by the Rev. Dr. Bellows, with Booth serving as best man. A friend, Bayard Taylor composed a sonnet for the occasion. Mary Silva Cosgrave, in a published lecture, wrote that Lilian knew of the poetry of Aldrich, whom she had assumed to be much older, but Booth, sometime before the party, explained to her: "he does not look 20 [he was actually 26]; he is short and blond and gay and brilliant; never had a wife, never had a child, never had anything, I guess, but the Muses, and poetical license."

Sarah Bolton in her anthology found Aldrich "cheerful in face, polished in manner, witty in conversation and brilliant in mind."

Writing in "Sarah Orne Jewett," Paula Blanchard's own description of Aldrich was that he was small in stature with blond curly hair parted in the middle, a ruddy complexion, and having nimble movements. She described his "darting wit," as effecting a birdlike air about him "though perhaps more of a bantam rooster than the drab little song bird." The latter reference was to Miss Jewett's affectionate nickname for Aldrich as a

---

time of this writer's visit on April 28, 2010.

[1] One reference lists date as November 18, 1865.

linnet.

"Unaccountably shy in large groups," opined Ms. Blanchard, "among friends he kept up a steady prattle of inspired foolishness and repartee."

According to C.A. Hazlett, writing in The Granite Monthly edition of March 1915, Aldrich's Grandfather Bailey (whom he erroneously dubbed "Nutter," his fictional name) was adverse to his grandson's selection of his wife. Upon having Lilian described to him as "a pretty New York belle," Bailey decided "she would be too extravagant for a man depending on his pen for his income." The eventual birth of twins, he sniffed, was another example of "just her extravagance." With the passage of time his attitude changed. Hazlett alludes to a letter the grandfather later wrote bearing a more positive attitude toward the match.

Mrs. Aldrich's sensitivities apparently were not considered by Hazlett since the article was printed a dozen years before she died.

In the September 1898 issue of "The Gentlewoman," Aldrich is described as being of medium height," thoroughly dignified," and dressing with the greatest care; "an American Frenchman," in personal appearance. Greenslet describes him as having "gray-blue eyes, and crisp, golden hair." A likeness in his 1863 book of poetry depicts his profile as having a long patrician nose and a nondescript chin.

Charles W. Chesnutt, one of his contributors to The Atlantic Monthly, described what others had termed blond tresses as "auburn-haired".

At the party, Lilian cajoled Booth into introducing them and thrilled at being able to "touch the hand that had penned words that burn." She had been particularly taken by the "Ballad of Babie Bell," which had achieved his first flush of success at 18 years of age, appearing in the poet's corner of local newspapers from Maine to Texas after its initial appearance in – of all things – The Journal of Commerce. In later years, as he matured, Aldrich expressed regret in having penned most of it, excepting only a few phrases. His virtual life-long friend, William Winter stated it enjoyed "world-wide circulation".

Less than two weeks after they were married, Aldrich was named editor of Every Saturday, a journal devoted to publishing the best of foreign periodical literature, which debuted in Boston January 1, 1866.

The couple's only children were identical twins: Charles, born just before Talbot, on September 17, 1868. Charles was named after Aldrich's uncle and Talbot after a good friend, Dr. Israel Tisdale Talbot, Mrs.

Aldrich's obstetrician. In a letter composed the day following the twins' birth, Aldrich wrote Dr. Talbot, apprising him of the favored decision.

Aldrich and James Russell Lowell had corresponded from time to time which no doubt prompted the latter to predict: "If they are proper twins, they will be one sentimental and t'other humorous," in a letter dated December 23, 1868.

In a letter written July 18, 1885, Aldrich notes that his sons have been under the tutorship of a Mr. Greene for the last two years "and have made marked advance." He noted that the pedagogue drilled the twins in Latin and found him to be "an excellent general scholar." Sarah Bolton said Aldrich's intentions were to prepare his sons for Harvard.

The artistic talents of Talbot, known as Tal, were evident early in life. As a child he sent his mother notes decorated with drawings, such as a flower, clock and type of clown, perhaps a court jester, or a harlequin. As an older lad he drew his mother a more sophisticated and detailed sketch of a steamboat.

Aldrich himself had a hand in their education - albeit sugarcoated. He had translated from the original French by Emile De La Bédollière "The Story of a Cat," set during the reign of King Louis XV. Published in 1879, its preface makes it clear for whose intent it was written:

"[This] charming story of Mother Michel and her cat was turned into English for the entertainment of two small readers at the writer's fireside . . . The ingenious and spirited series of silhouettes with which Mr. Hopkins has enriched the text is the translator's only plea for presenting in book form so slight a performance as his own part of the work."

In at least one letter reference, Aldrich recalls playing ball with his boys, whom he called Charley and Tal.

A month before the twins' seventh birthday anniversary, Aldrich wrote them from Europe. In it, he displayed (presumably in jest) his not uncommon pomposity in describing Robert Burns, whose birthplace he had visited:

"He wrote verses, just as your father does; only his verses were not quite so good as your father's!"

His son Charles became a member of the First Corps of Cadets with the Massachusetts Volunteer Militia.

On January 24, 1893 in a letter to the University Club in Boston, Aldrich discloses that one of his 24-year-old sons is "very ill," but does not name which one or disclose his ailment. Earlier, on December 30, 1889, in another letter to a financier, he had disclosed his own suffering from a bad case of what he termed "la grippe" and said that his head "was aching in such a fashion as to give me the idea that I had got a misfit skull, the skull of some smaller man – it was so tight across the brows."

In a letter from his home in Boston dated January 6, 1901, Aldrich declines a social invitation explaining, "I am all tangled up in all kinds of engagements growing out of my son's marriage. "The Twains are to come to us on the 14th and other guests are to follow them."

On December 25, 1900, Charles Frost Aldrich married Maria Louise Richards (nee Alexander), a widow with a young daughter named Beverly Richards and son, Junius Alexander Richards, according to Charles A. Winchester, 86, the married couples' grandson, of Dublin, New Hampshire, in responding on September 12, 2010 to this writer's query[1]. The bride was born in 1869, Staten Island, New York Her first

---

[1] The Charles Frost Aldrich – Maria Louise Richards marriage produced a daughter, Lillian, born December 31, 1901. Her name was spelled with three ls, unlike that of her paternal grandmother. Lillian married a banker, John G. Winchester and they had a son, Charles A., the source of this information, whose daughter Ann Conway is said to live in Peterborough, N.H. Charles A. Winchester's parents lived in New York City and Scarsdale, N.Y. They divorced in 1930 and his mother took up residence in Boston and her summer home in Dublin, N.H. where her son continued to live. Following the death of his maternal grandfather, his grandmother moved to 444 Beacon Street, Boston.

husband, whom she married in 1891 died eight years later. On July 2, 2012 her travel trunk surfaced in an antique shop in Amherst, New Hampshire, according to Gail Johnson, a former Strawbery Banke interpreter and co-researcher. She said Charles' widow traveled extensively into the 1940s. Her passport showed her to be a "handsome dark-haired woman."

Downloaded on July 5, 2012 from nutfieldgenealogy.blogspot.com was information that the trunk was taken aboard the White Star Line the SS Cedric in 1929, on the Boston-Liverpool run, Mrs. Charles Frost Aldrich occupied suite 53. The blog cites her membership in the Colonial Dames Society as a descendant of Mayflower passenger William Bradford, as well as her inclusion in the Boston Social Register.

When Charles A. Winchester was born, his great-grandmother Lilian Woodman Aldrich, although still alive "never visited" he said, nor was his mother subsequently known to have paid a call on the elderly woman who died in 1927 at age 86. According to a newspaper obituary at that time (likely the Boston Herald) Mrs. Aldrich collapsed while playing bridge at the home of Mr. and Mrs. W.O. Fuller of Rockland, Maine. She had continued to live at the 59 Mount Vernon St., Boston address. Her son Talbot, who resided in an 1878 four-story townhouse at 34 Fairfield St., Boston, arranged for funeral services at Mt. Auburn Chapel, Cambridge, Massachusetts.

Charles suffered from tuberculosis. Though he had hemorrhaged in September, 1901, by December of that year he had rallied sufficiently for his father to write a colleague about it. Aldrich wrote his son "is holding his own, and we are encouraged about him," predicting however that "he probably will be held . . . for many months." Charles died at age 35 about two-and-half years after the tuberculosis was diagnosed (the conflicting old house book stated "one year later" than his marriage date of 1900, which in itself is in conflict) at Saranac Lake, New York, on March 6, 1904.

According to Marshall S. Berdan following Charles' death, Aldrich never once returned to The Porcupine, the house he built to be near his son. Berdan, in his Adirondack Line Online article, notes the property was "down the street from the Trudeau[1] Sanatorium," where Charles was a patient. Hours before Charles' death,

[1] Dr. Edward Livingstone Trudeau in 1885 built the first one-room cottage at what became the Adirondack Cottage Sanatorium, as per the Summer 2005 edition of New England Ancestors.

Aldrich wrote Mark Twain that his son's "minutes were numbered." Charles is buried in Mount Auburn Cemetery, Cambridge, Massachusetts, and three years later, his father was entombed next to him. Twain had been instrumental in finding a lot seller and an architect for which Aldrich was able to build The Porcupine.

Talbot Bailey Aldrich married Eleanor Lovell Little (1884-1978) of Salem, Massachusetts, on June 30, 1906. He acquired the title of major[1] and was an artist, who illustrated his mother's book, "The Shadow of the

---

[1] Jonathan Aldrich, of Cape Elizabeth, Maine, told this writer on October 5, 2002 that his grandfather was "always called 'The Major'," but could not elucidate. Whether the title was achieved through active military service could not be determined, since a family tale that Talbot served in the Army during a war with Mexico is speculative, in light of when the 19th century contentious incidents occurred. Possibly he participated in the Spanish-American War. He did hold the title of major in the Ancient and Honorable Company of Massachusetts and served as president of the Sons of the American Revolution Massachusetts Society. According to Talbot's grandnephew, Charles A. Winchester of Dublin, New Hampshire: "Talbot Aldrich served [principally in the first decade of the 20th Century] as a major on the staff of Governors Curtis Guild, Sr. and Eben S. Draper. He represented the Milton-Canton-Westwood district in the [Massachusetts] legislature from 1920-22."

Flowers." He also worked in oils, painting an exquisite study of a choir boy – probably his son - in a bright red cassock and white surplice, as well as a view of Little Acres in Hudson, Massachusetts, which Nina Fletcher Little, descendent of an apparent in-law, describes as "our first small house in the country as it looked in the late 1920s."

Knowing he helped his mother create his father's memorial museum, Talbot is also said to have helped paint the red speckles on the breasts of the birds on the wallpaper in an effort to duplicate that which might have hung in his father's boyhood hall room bedchamber. Talbot's great-grandson, Thomas Hugh Aldrich, in an interview October 5, 2002, said the family still retains many of his great-grandfather's paintings.

Talbot and Eleanor had a son Bailey Aldrich, born April 23, 1907 in Boston, who became a United States Circuit Court of Appeals judge. It is ironic that his mother forbade the boy from reading novels, according to Bailey's son, Jonathan, presumably even those penned by his illustrious grandfather Thomas! The judge donated his Great-grandfather Bailey's main house to the Strawbery Banke Museum on August 5, 1979. Included were its furnishings and the adjacent brick museum though *its* contents were not turned over to Strawbery

Banke until December 1986.

The Houghton Library at Harvard has an undated letter from Eleanor to her mother-in-law. Identified as Call# b MS AM 1429, it states in part:

"Dear Lily, You always say you do not like to write letters but you always write just the right kind, telling everything that interests and that other persons are apt to omit…I was glad to know that you had the Walkers, Tal had not thought to mention that they were coming and it was a real nightmare to me to think of you alone those nights. I was much relieved by the news in your letter. I cannot realize at all that Miss Reid has gone and that I shall not find her sitting in her little room…I can't bear to think that a void she has left in your life. Her position in the household you may fill, but her friendship with its interests and sympathy and devoted care of you, you can never replace. It was wonderful that she did not have to live away from you except these last few days."

The letter had to have been written after Miss Reid was listed among the household staff in the 1910 census. The "Walkers" may have been an allusion to J. Albert and Arthur W. Walker, who in the 1905 Portsmouth City Directory lived at 9 Middle Street. The earliest reference uncovered by this writer on Elizabeth Reid, was in the

1890 census. Born in 1844 in England, she was identified as the housekeeper in the Aldrich's Ponkapog home in Canton, Massachusetts. There were four additional servants by then: Margaret McCarthy, 25, a native of the Bay State who had been recommended to the Aldriches by the Henry Pierce household staff[1] and the following ethnic Irish James W. Hannon, 25, the butler; Susan McInery, 32 and Bessie Eames, 22.

Servants in the Aldrich household at Ponkapog ten years earlier were both Irish-born, Margaret Murphy, 26 and Helena Lucy, 23. Mrs. Aldrich's mother, Mary Woodman, was listed among the resident family.

By 1910, three years after her husband's death, Mrs. Aldrich was living in Boston with Miss Reid and three other servants: Florence Reardon, 24, Massachusetts-born and listed as a chauffeur (?); Margaret McCarthy, who had been in her service for at least 20 years and Irish-born Anna Farrell, 36.

According to Trudi Wallace Olivetti of Swamscot, Massachusetts, who visited the Thomas Bailey Aldrich Memorial Museum complex on August 16, 2011,

---

[1] Her grand-nephew David Crawley, who lives in Canton, visited the Aldrich Museum in Strawbery Banke May 26, 2014 and supplied the family relationship.

Talbot's wife, Eleanor died in 1978. Mrs. Olivetti recalled her family renting one of her cottages in Tenants Harbor, Maine in the 1940s. Eleanor, helped found the Tenants Harbor library, but strangely would not allow her son Bailey to read fiction. Mrs. Olivetti recalled that Eleanor, who drove a green Plymouth, once went for a swim but had difficulty swimming back.

"I scampered down the stairs and pulled her in," said Mrs. Olivettti, who was in her 20s at the time.

She also shed light on the "rose-covered cottage" that Lilian Aldrich wrote so obtusely about. It indeed was in Tenants Harbor and was being rented for a time in the 20th century by Eleanor's friend, a Mrs. Logan.

III. ALDRICH'S VARIOUS KNOWN RESIDENCES

1. Born at 60 (a/k/a 61) Court Street, Portsmouth in what is now known as the Laighton House, and lived there six weeks.

2. From age six weeks he lived with his maternal grandparents in Portsmouth at 40 (later renumbered 45, and in 1877 as 51) Court Street. The house is currently listed as 386 Court Street, according to John Mead Howell's "The Architectural Heritage of the Piscataqua." There is some question as to just how long Aldrich lived there at the onset. Ferris Greenslet, in his Aldrich biography, claims the boy left Portsmouth at the tender age of 18 months to hopscotch the nation. In an apparent attempt at hyperbole, Aldrich himself writes his parents lived in every state in the union. Despite Greenslet's and Aldrich's assertions, this writer has not been able to find a single shred of evidence linking the Aldrich family to any other community until they moved to New York years later.[1]

3. From age four to age nine (1841-46) he lived with his parents in at least two nearby residences in New York City, one was at 941 North Moore Street, around the corner from Hudson Street, in a neighborhood known as lower Broadway. During this period Aldrich returned to Portsmouth annually for long summer vacations and presumably other shorter visits.

4. From age nine to age 12 (1846-49) he lived with his parents in New Orleans, Louisiana. The last address, at the time of his father's death was a waterfront property at 91 Tchoupitoulas Street. According to a former New Orleans resident, it is an old Indian name.

---

[1] John Mayer, former Strawbery Banke Museum curator, who had amassed a considerable amount of Aldrich material, responded on August 21, 2006 to this complier's query as to whether he could shed any light on Aldrich's whereabouts during that time. "[You] asked me if I had in my notes where Thomas Bailey Aldrich and his family were between 1838-1841. It's a good question. That was the transitional time when his father was involved in some kind of business but we haven't found out where or what," wrote Mayer in an e-mail.

5. From age 12 to 16 (1849-52), he lived in his grandfather's house in Portsmouth. He returned periodically for visits, usually for long stretches in the summer, until the grandfather died in 1870.

These extended vacations were confirmed in a March 1915 reminiscence in The Granite Monthly, a New Hampshire magazine, by C.A. Hazlett, with whom he had corresponded in adulthood.

6. From 1852-65, he lived in the home of his uncle and aunt, Charles and Caroline Frost at 105 Clinton Street – or Clinton Place as his hand-written letterhead once indicated - which later became 133 Eighth Street, immediately opposite to the northern end of Macdougal Street, in the Greenwich Village section of New York City. His bedroom was a small hall room on the third floor rear. It is interesting that Aldrich continued to live there for some 10 years after leaving his uncle's employ, although by 1860 – or perhaps earlier - his mother had returned to Portsmouth to live with her parents. Aldrich revisited that New York house for old times' sake in the late 1890s, but found it "mangy" and "disreputable," and declined to enter. By 1909 the year his long-time friend William Winter published his memoir "Old Friends," the house was "occupied by tradesmen, and its aspect, like that of its neighborhood, is changed."

7. Edwin Booth's home on 19th Street in New York City. Aldrich lived there with Booth in 1865 following the assassination of President Abraham Lincoln by Booth's younger brother, John Wilkes Booth. In doing so, Aldrich helped Booth through the crisis. It is ironic that earlier in 1865, Edwin Booth rescued President Lincoln's son, Robert, who had slipped between the wheels of a moving train in a New Jersey station.

8. His first residence as a married man in late 1865 was a boarding house on Hancock Street "on the summit" of Beacon Hill, Boston.

9. A four-story townhouse at 84 Pinckney Street, Boston, acquired in December 1866, and lived in by the Aldriches from the spring of 1867 until the birth of the twins on September 17, 1868. Ferris Greenslet wrote the Aldriches used the cook's seven-year-old daughter, Lizzie, as a handmaiden, to greet at the door and assist at table, and once had this child offer in her little lisp some wine and fruit to a delighted Charles Dickens, who was said to have first visited Boston in 1842.

10. A townhouse on Charles Street, Boston after the birth of the twins, which they occupied for two years until moving out of the city, and returned to briefly. The boys' health is said to have prompted the initial move.

11. In 1872, after moving out of the city, the Aldriches leased James Russell Lowell's home called "Elmwood" in Cambridge, Massachusetts, until the owner's return from Europe two years later; then they moved back to their home on Charles Street which they had been renting out in the interim. While in Cambridge, they were neighbors of D. W. Howells, who immediately preceded Aldrich as editor-in-chief of The Atlantic Monthly. On November 12, 1904, Ferris Greenslet, who was to become Aldrich's posthumous biographer, wrote him from Boston for anecdotes pertaining to Lowell, whose biography he was contemplating.

12. After a brief return to their Charles Street home they moved in 1874 to a remodeled farmhouse in a more rural area of the Bay State. Dubbed Redman Farm, it was located 12 miles south of Boston, in the Blue Hills, overlooking the Neponset marshes known as Ponkapog, an old Indian reservation, in what is now Canton, Massachusetts. There was train service to that area at that time and what Aldrich termed "an ancient equipage" for visitors to take from the station to his home for which he had secured a five-year lease. In a letter to his friend, Bayard Taylor he explained his choice thusly:

"You ask me why I bury myself in these wilds. I was never so comfortable . . . I've 125 chickens! I have butter that would cost you a dollar per pound in New York that you cannot get at any price."

According to Howard S.Whitley's "History of Ponkapoag [sic] Camp," Aldrich went fishing with his twin sons Tal and Charlie for perch and pickerel and entertained Mark Twain there.

In the 1880 census besides the Aldriches and their sons, living there were his mother-in-law and two servants, Margaret Murphy and Helena Lacy.

13. After Samuel Clemens/Mark Twain had his 25-room Gothic Revival brick home built in 1874 in Hartford, Connecticut, (he had had temporary residence in that city since 1871) Aldrich used it as a halfway station between Boston and New York. Twain kept the property, with its Tiffany interiors, where he worked as well as lived until 1891.

14. In 1878, Aldrich spent the summer in Swampscott, Massachusetts, along Nahent Bay.

William H. Rideing, in his 1910 magazine piece,

notes upon leaving a party in Newton, he and Aldrich repaired to the latter's seaside cottage "on Lynn Terrace," likely the same residence Aldrich took in 1878 and perhaps in other seasons as well. Aldrich's poem "Lynn Terrace" is considered by Greenslet to be one of his finest. Sarah K. Bolton in her Aldrich biography cites the poem as inspired by a large red wooden villa on the seashore "at Lynn." Since Swampscott borders Lynn – which was not separated from Swampscott until 1853 - that could explain the discrepancy. She said to date (1887) he had spent 17 summers in that villa except on those occasions when he was in Europe.

15. "The Crags," built in the summer of 1893 at Tenants Harbor, on the coast of St. George peninsula, a wooded point east of Brunswick on the western edge of Penobscot Bay in Maine.

Whether this particular "nest" is the rose cottage to which Mrs. Aldrich refers is uncertain[1] , although one with that description remained in the family name in that location well into the 20th century. Aldrich writes an acquaintance the following spring he is "to take

---

[1] Mrs. Olivetti however appears to have confirmed the properties are one and the same as noted earlier in this book.

possession of my little cottage May 1 [1894]." Sarah Orne Jewett, the poetess, spent a long weekend here in July, 1895 to see for herself what Aldrich deemed magical.

16. According to Marshall S. Berdan, writing in Adirondack Life Online, in the winter of 1901-02, the Aldriches rented a house known as Highland Manor in Saranac Lake, New York, to be near their son, Charles, admitted to the Trudeau Sanatorium following a sudden hemorrhage of the lungs in September 1901. Ferris Greenslet, Aldrich's biographer, noted the father found his son "very thin and white and feeble. At times I have to turn my eyes away, but my heart keeps looking at him." Greenslet noted Aldrich depicted the temporary lodgings thusly: "We've taken an overgrown cottage on the outskirts of the town, which at night looks like a cluster of stars dropped into the hollow. The young Aldriches (presumably Charles' wife, daughter and stepchildren) have a cottage near by."

17. Since Charles' consumption necessitated time in the Adriondacks, where the Trudeau Sanatorium and several other residences operated as tubercular asylums, Aldrich decided to have his own country home - known as a retreat – built near Mt. Pisgah, in Saranac Lake. Called The Porcupine[1], it was where he kept a dog, named Buster, which he claimed was so dumb it kept getting porcupine quills in its snout. Berdan noted Aldrich purchased a four-and-a-half acre plot in the spring of 1902, down the street from the sanatorium. His plan was to spend at least half a year there annually to be close to his son and his son's family. For several weeks he superintended the building of the Adirondack shingle-style gambrel-roofed manse designed by William L. Coulter. Situated along what was known as Millionaires Row, it has six gables on its two-and-a-half story frame and currently overlooks a three-acre garden adjacent to a forest. The Porcupine, whose address is 147 Park Avenue, is currently a picturesque bed-and-breakfast inn with eight bedrooms. Its present proprietors Barbara and Jerry Connolly have retained the name dubbed by Aldrich.

---

[1] So named because in those days writers were sometimes known as "quill pushers".

18. At 59 Mount Vernon Street, Beacon Hill, Boston, Massachusetts, which he purchased in 1883[1] and where he died. In the September 1898 issue of "The Gentlewoman," the house was described as a "white mansion." Sarah K. Bolton depicted it as a four-story red brick building with a white marble doorway, in a block of houses. She noted the town house contained a 3,000-volume library. Mark Twain was known to have visited him here.

19. According to Marshall S. Berdan, writing in Adirondack Life Online, following Charles' death in 1904, Aldrich moved temporarily to a residence in York Harbor, Maine "to escape from the memories associated with Boston and the Crags." There's no little irony in its proximity to his boyhood home in the Puddle Dock district of Portsmouth, New Hampshire, which he had

---

[1] This contradicts Samuel Clemens' autobiography in which Henry Lillie Pierce, former mayor of Boston, is supposed to have *given* Aldrich that house – in which he (Pierce) coincidentally died - plus a cottage by the sea (perhaps the one in Swampscott, Massachusetts). Still another source lists the house as being willed by Pierce to the Aldrich family among other legacies. Indications are Mrs. Aldrich would take full advantage of Pierce's largess.

left more-or-less permanently 52 years earlier. Berdan said Aldrich devoted his time in York Harbor working on the dramatization of his narrative poem "Judith and Holofernes."

IV. MILITARY ASPIRATIONS

Aldrich had expected an appointment in the military, but hopes proved in vain.

On April 26, 1861, he wrote to New Hampshire Governor Icabod Goodwin, offering his services as aide-de-camp to the colonel in command of the New Hampshire regiment.

"I most respectfully solicit your interest in procuring me the appointment. If the power of placing me on the staff does not lie directly in your own hands, I am sure that your friendly influence if you have time to use it, can accomplish my desire," he said. C.A. Hazlett claimed in a March 1915 article in The Granite Monthly he was given Aldrich's letter by Governor Goodwin, explaining, "it came too late for the governor to grant the commission."

Aldrich also applied for a position on the staff of General F. W. Lander, an old friend, according to Caroline Ticknor, writing in "Glimpses of Authors."

General Lander did send a telegram to Aldrich at Portsmouth offering him a staff appointment with the rank of lieutenant. However, Aldrich was not in town at that time and the telegram remained unopened. The appointment then went to Aldrich's former friend Fitz-James O'Brien, subsequently mortally wounded on February 26, 1862, in a skirmish with Confederate cavalry. The shoulder joint of his left arm had been smashed into fragments, and O'Brien died from the complications and lockjaw on April 5, 1862 at Cumberland, Virginia.[1]

According to William Winter, when Henry Clapp, their old boss on The Saturday Press, heard of the tragedy, he quipped: "Aldrich I see, has been shot in O'Brien's shoulder." Explaining the reason for the macabre statement, Winter said that "the old cynic did not like either of them." Albert R. Waud, an artist of the day, told Winter that O'Brien had expressed a premonition of his death en route to Harper's Ferry to join his contingent.

"He had a presentiment that he should be shot before long," said Waud. "He would not be rallied out of it, but remarked that he was content; and, when we parted, said goodbye as cheerfully as need be."

---

[1] Another reference states it was April 6, 1862 in Cumberland, Maryland.

Duel Challenge

O'Brien, the talented but tempestuous writer, once challenged Aldrich to a duel.[1] Both had at one time been the closest of friends and they even roomed together for a week in the New York home of Aldrich's uncle, Charles Frost. William Winter, in his memoir, recalled O'Brien bedding down in his own New York digs on Varick Street for a couple nights in the autumn of 1860. He wrote O'Brien was "on the rock [destitute]" at the time, and made use of the shelter by penning a work which he sold to Harper's Magazine then squandered the proceeds by dispensing free drinks to all and sundry at the famed Delmonico's Restaurant[2].

Aldrich, eight years younger, declined the writer's challenge, stating that the "rules did not permit me to duel with one who owed him money." He had loaned O'Brien $35 (another reference states $40) to pay a

---

[1] John Brougham, a comedian of the day, was said to have maintained that O'Brien never cared much for any person with whom he did not quarrel.

[2] Whose exorbitant prices made even New Hampshire Governor Ichabod Goodwin's wife Sarah, blanch.

pressing bill. In his youth O'Brien had squandered an 8,000-pound (possibly tantamount to $40,000) bequest, used instead to host a dinner party at one of his favorite haunts, Delmonico's.

In a letter dated September 7, 1880 to his friend William Winter, Aldrich confesses that he could not immediately recall the year in which O'Brien, a wastrel, had been taken in his uncle's house to share his tiny third floor rear bedchamber. Winter recalled O'Brien wrote his story "What Was It?" during his stay with Aldrich.

"I was reluctant to give up the idea of writing the O'Brien reminiscences," he wrote, "but I am obliged to give it up. I lack the time not only to do the actual writing, but to verify the many dates I should have to mention."

Aldrich did recall that from 1858 to 1859 "O'Brien and I . . . never let a day pass without meeting." They first met in 1853; a year after O'Brien had arrived in New York.

"When I first knew O'Brien, he was 'trimming the wick' of The Lantern, which went out shortly afterward," Aldrich recalled about that publication.

He wrote Winter that in 1862 the year of O'Brien's death he had prepared an article on the tempestuous poet and science fiction writer for Harper's Weekly, but it remained unpublished and "in a drawer of my work table for two or three years afterward. [It] was either lost or destroyed at the time I moved to Boston."

There apparently was a period of relative affluence in New York for O'Brien. According to George Arnold, a poet of the day: "When I first knew O'Brien, in 1856-57, he had elegant rooms; a large and valuable library; piles of manuscripts; dressing-cases; pictures; a wardrobe of much splendor; and all sorts of knick-knackery, such as young bachelors love to collect."

One of O'Brien's highly regarded pieces was the long narrative poem "The Sewing Bird," published September, 1860 in Harper's New Monthly Magazine and lavishly illustrated. In it O'Brien raises the social conscience through an impoverished seamstress working in a shabby room when a sewing bird, a device to hold cloth fast while it is being worked, comes alive and transports her to a dry goods shop depicting only faultlessly-dressed effete male clerks. Her yearning to achieve such a clerical position presages women's liberation.

Nearly two decades earlier in the fall of 1861 Aldrich applied for work as a war correspondent with Horace Greeley's New York Tribune, and saw some of the realities of war. When he returned to New York in 1862, he became literary advisor to a publishing firm, and then in January, 1863, managing editor of The Illustrated News.

As a correspondent for the Tribune, in October 1861, Aldrich covered the Civil War on horseback with the Union Army of the Potomac, near Washington, D.C.

It apparently was so cold in that part of Virginia, that, upon sharing a blanket with a Private Maguire, from a New York regiment, he declared the coverlet was worth "$50.00 an inch!" Aldrich, who would later recoil at being misidentified as having Irish ancestry, wrote a poem in the man's honor, entitled: "Says Private Maguire," published in his volume "Songs of the Soldiers," in 1864. Written in what he thought was the vernacular of an unschooled Irishman, it speaks of Maguire resenting the life of officers, but includes the couplet:

Faith now, it's not that I'm afther (sic) complainin'
I'm spillin' to meet ye, Jeff Davis, Esquire!

Out of his war experience, also came several short stories: "Quite So," "Shaw Memorial Ode" and "The White Feather."

Although "Fredericksburg" is said to be considered

among his most famous sonnets which commemorates a December 13, 1862 battle at that Virginia community, it was composed some time after his stint at the Tribune.

While still a correspondent, in a letter dated October 30, 1861 on file at the Houghton Library, Harvard, he wrote his mother of his experiences.

"I have just returned from a long ride into the enemy's country. I have been on horseback two days and two nights... but I did get out of the saddle to sleep. What a strange time I had of it" he wrote, noting that he and Ned House, a Tribune colleague, joined a Union general and his staff on reconnaissance "when I got separated from the party."

He related as to how House made it back to Washington having given him up for lost.

"Suddenly I found myself alone in a tangle of dense forest and unknown woods. Close on the rebel lines, not knowing quite what direction, without a guide, and nothing to eat – you may imagine that I wished myself on the harmless banks of the Piscataqua," he disclosed in a bid for maternal sympathy. Aldrich continued the narrative, waxing even more poetic:

"To crown it all, a moonless night was darkening down on the terrible stillness, and as the darkness grew, I caught glimpses of lurid campfires here and here – a kind of goblin glare which lent an indiscernible and unpleasantness to the scene. Whether these were the campfires of friend or foe, I had no means of telling. I put spurs to my horse and dashed on," he wrote.

Eventually he fell asleep and upon awakening spotted the dome of the nation's capital in the morning light.

"Here I am, a year older in looks," he concluded.

This writer has been unable to find any dispatches from Aldrich to his newspaper during this period. However, a colleague, George Washburn Smalley (1832-1916), who married the love of Aldrich's bachelorhood Phoebe Garnant (the Smalleys separated decades later in 1898) is among the best known of war correspondents. His reputation as an ace reporter for that same paper, the Tribune, is based on his having witnessed the Battle of Antietam on September 17, 1862. Twice grazed by bullets while covering Union General George Brinton McClellan's victory there, Smalley, a Yale graduate, managed to board a train bound for New York and file his copy, after he had found telegraph lines jammed in several towns in Virginia and Maryland. In his day Smalley was considered the dean of American correspondents. Part of this information is based on an interview given by James McPherson, Pulitzer-prize-winning historian on the National Public Radio Program

"Fresh Air," broadcast June 22, 2004.

Sylvanus Cadwallader, chief correspondent for the New York Herald is credited with establishing formal arrangements in which newspapers from the North and South could easily be exchanged on a daily basis[1].

---

[1] Source: "A Bohemian Brigade, The Civil War Correspondents," by James M. Perry, John Wiley & sons, publishers, New York 2000.

V. WRITING AND EDITING JOBS

Henry C. Vedder in his book "American Writers of Today," explained the situation struggling, budding writers faced in those days:

"Knickerbocker's and Putnam's and Goedy's were the only periodicals then published which could accept and pay for even an occasional contribution. Mr. Aldrich [was] compelled therefore, to look for some semi-literary occupations that would ensure his living while he wrote.

This he found for a time in a publishing house, for which he acted as reader of manuscripts submitted for publications and as a proof-reader also."

Aldrich's first regular writing job was as junior literary agent for the Evening Mirror in New York in 1855. During his employ of less than one year, he reviewed Henry Wadsworth Longfellow's "Hiawatha" favorably, shortly before his 19th birthday anniversary. It's interesting to note there was indirect correspondence between Longfellow and Aldrich, via the latter's friend William Winter in 1855, three years before the pair began corresponding directly. Winter, in effect, became the go-between. The recognition of each other was based on Winter's forwarding to Longfellow extracts of some of his letters written by Aldrich, and the latter's responses to that Harvard professor's reactions.

Less than a year after joining the Evening Mirror, Aldrich became sub-editor of the Home Journal in 1856, receiving a submission from his friend Fitz-James O'Brien, under a playful cover letter. According to Lilian Aldrich, writing in "Crowding Memories," Nathanial Parker Willis gave him the position once held by Edgar Allan Poe. Aldrich held that post until 1859, when he quit ostensibly because he – an ardent pipe smoker – had not been permitted to do so on the job.

William Winter, his near life-long friend, quotes Aldrich about his inchoate experience in the world of journalism.

"I had no idea of what 'work' is 'til I became sub[editor]," he wrote. "I have found that reading proof and writing articles on uninteresting subjects . . . no joke. The cry for 'more copy' rings through my ears in dream, and hosts of little phantom printers' devils walk over my body all night and prick me with sharp-pointed types! Last evening I fell asleep in my armchair and dreamed that they were about to put ***me*** 'to press'."

The bohemian Saturday Press was established October 29, 1858, and Aldrich at age 21 was hired at its onset to write book reviews, becoming its associate editor before leaving the publication three months later in early 1859[1]. His friend, Fitz-James O'Brien, was engaged at the same time to write theatrical commentary, but left after a few weeks. The Saturday Press was a vivacious journal, which enjoyed the admiration and support of the young literary men of the country, but unfortunately it expired in December 1860.

Among the bohemian group who helped establish the Saturday Press was Bayard Taylor (1825-1878), a poet, essayist and traveler who, in 1850 had won P. T. Barnum's contest for a song welcoming Jenny Lind to America. Although he later eschewed his prize-winning lyrics, he mused they might eventually save him from oblivion. He was a professor of German at Cornell from 1870-77 and United States Minister to Germany in 1878, the year of his death. Also, in the group was Edmund Clarence (perhaps better known as E.C.) Stedman (1833-1908), a poet, journalist and critic, and a war

[1] Reference dates may be in error since it is unlikely Aldrich held overlapping positions during part of his employment at both the Home Journal and Saturday Press.

correspondent for the New York World, during the Civil War. He wrote books on American literature. Both became good friends of Aldrich.

Others included William Winter, of course, who – as a teenage writer for the Boston Transcript first knew of Aldrich when assigned to write a book notice for the latter's "The Bells"; R. H. Stoddard, whose New York home served as a salon for the *literati*, and a group of lesser figures who constituted the artist colony of the time.

This writer can find no reference to any employment for Aldrich during 1860. There is a reference to his becoming a literary advisor in 1862 to a publishing firm, most likely Rudd & Carleton which had published his poetry book, "Pampinea . . ." in 1861. The reason this cannot be stated with certainty is though it is known he worked in that capacity for that publishing house the actual date is unknown to this writer.

As previously noted, Aldrich joined the Illustrated News, a New York pictorial weekly, in January 1863, in the capacity of managing editor. With P. T. Barnum as co-founder, it had premiered 10 years earlier on January 1, 1853. Barnum had appointed as its first editor, Rufus Wilmot Griswold, whom Irving Wallace, in his Barnum biography "The Fabulous Showman," described as "untrustworthy."

The publication, while tainted as a "rag sheet," full of reprints, soon reached a circulation of 150,000.

"Because Barnum [and his partners] were too busy to devote full time to the [periodical], and too close-fisted, [it] soon languished," said Wallace, noting that nonetheless after a year or so, Barnum et al., "managed to sell out to a Boston publishing firm without loss."

When Aldrich came on board he found work there "monotonous and unceasing," according to Ferris Greenslet, his biographer, who cited his covering a Russian ball as an example presumably of the former.

A traumatic assignment developed when, armed with only a tablet and pencil, Aldrich commenced sketching an assembling mob protesting the drafting of men for the Army in the Civil War. On July 13, 1863, he was spotted by one of the mob's leaders, who shouted: "Down with him! Kill him!"

In the foray, Aldrich's wrist was badly cut and he was disabled from writing for some time. It was months before he could pick up a pen or pencil. He stopped working for the Illustrated News later that same year, which was probably not long before the 11-year-old publication folded.

According to "New York", an anthology published by

Little Brown and Company in 1985, the draft riots ran for about four days that July 1863. Mobs demolished draft headquarters and sought out African-Americans, who were chased, beaten and even lynched - hung on trees or lampposts. The Colored Orphan Asylum on Fifth Avenue, near 43rd Street was set afire. The superintendent and matrons managed to lead the more than 200 children out by the rear of the wooden building. They found temporary shelter in police stations before being ferried to Blackwell's Island and refuge. Federal troops were summoned from Pennsylvania. The toll was the killing or wounding of more than 1,000 people with property damage estimated at a million dollars.

Less than a month later and presumably while still recuperating from the attack against him, Aldrich suffered a severe bout of sunstroke. Writing his Uncle Charles, who with his family and Aldrich's mother had taken a boat trip to the mountains and seashore, he detailed his illness thusly:

"Samuel Thomkins [a friend] has been staying with me nights and saved me, I think from a brain fever by keeping wet towels on my head...the city is virtually roasted. You escaped just in time."

In Boston:

In 1865 he accepted the position of editor of Every Saturday, a Boston publication, and continued to be employed there until 1874. Although he received the official offer on November 17, he apparently held high hopes, for in a letter dated two days earlier to a man named Graham (otherwise unidentified) Aldrich spoke of having his library boxed in preparation for his move to Boston from New York.

From 1873 to 1903, he published novels and travel sketches and edited "The Young Folks Literary Selections from the Choicest Literature of All Lands," a total of 20 volumes. In 1875[1] he wrote "The Easy Chair," column in Harper's Magazine, as a fill-in for the regular columnist George W. Curtis, who was ailing.

From 1881 to 1890, Aldrich assumed the editorship of The Atlantic Monthly, which was launched in 1857. Its offices were located in a four-story building in Boston. In a March 8, 1881 letter to his longtime friend, William Winter, he expressed his thoughts about the

---

[1] In William Winter's recollection, Aldrich served as temporary replacement in 1873 when Curtis suffered a breakdown and rendered unable to work for several months.

lofty position:

"The editorial chair of The Atlantic Monthly is not the piece of furniture I would select for comfort . . . I don't have time to breathe."

In this high-profile position, Aldrich was besieged by tyros and professionals alike. An example is no less a personage than Bret Harte, writer of western sagas.

Writing from Glasgow, Scotland on April 17, 1884, Harte, while acquainted with Aldrich, had not realized he had become that respected publication's editor-in-chief and shamefacedly – albeit humorously – solicited to have not only his work published in the magazine but those of unnamed colleagues.

He became the literary advisor[1] for the publishing firm of Derby & Jackson, which had published his first book of poetry "The Bells." A letter Aldrich wrote dated April 29, 1886 terms that post as "reader." Regardless of official title, it nevertheless was held while he was still editor of The Atlantic Monthly. At the very least to this writer, it presages a potential conflict of interest.

---

[1] In Sarah Bolton's profile of Aldrich, the position is "assistant reader".

Work and Work Habits

Aldrich's first known published work was "Santonio," printed in the Portsmouth Journal, June 21, 1851, when he was just 14. The poem included these opening lines:

The warrior stood beside his dying steed,
And at his feet his broken sabre lay,
On every side, he saw his comrades dead
And he alone could tell of warlike deeds,
Of dying messages and slaughtered men.

In 1852 at age 16 Aldrich went to work for his Uncle Charles Frost in his uncle's counting house, at 146 Pearl Street, New York City. A counting house is said to be a building, room or office in which a banker, trader or manufacturer keeps records and transacts business. Frost, described by William Winter as a "portly merchant" was in 1860 director of the Concord & Portsmouth Railroad.

The teenage Aldrich was tutored and went to night school. In the Greenslet biography, there is a sarcastic reference by his Uncle Charles Frost to his nephew having studied Spanish on company time. By and large however there is a paucity of information as to a more comprehensive course of study. He knew French - for Madame Marie Thérèse de Solins Blanc, the French translator of his books wrote to him in that language. Sarah K. Bolton, in her profile of Aldrich noted that the youth "liked Latin and French, but not mathematics". Eventually he would study Italian and wrote he planned to learn German during the summer of 1877.

As a budding poet he waited in vain in the waiting room of the publisher of a Boston magazine and eventually spotted a ledger in the room. In it, he took it upon himself to write: "Don't forget to accept Aldrich's poem," and left the unnamed work there. Subsequently Aldrich did receive a check from the publisher, but it was more for Aldrich's cheek than his work, since the poem was never published.

Once, when Aldrich did have a poem published while still a teenager he was proud of the $15 he received for it, but his Uncle Charles Frost was not, since it probably represented a week's wages or more, and his uncle retorted with: "Why don't you send the damned fool one every day?"

Despite that outburst, Aldrich expressed fondness for his uncle.

"I am one of his family and he has been to me a

brother and a father. I enjoy the lofty and richer pleasures of life keenly, and the love of beauty in every form has become a part of my soul," he wrote in a letter to William Winter, a fellow teenager. In that same letter he stated his financial philosophy: "I value money only because it buys books."

He found the duties in his uncle's counting house not arduous enough to stop his creative writing. According to Ferris Greenslet, Aldrich declared later in life that he "wrote a lyric or two every day before going downtown," to the office building of his uncle, whom he once described as having a "shockingly bluff manner [but] displaying a heart as sensitive as a child's and as sympathetic as a woman's – for those he loved."

Working during the day his evenings were spent with an aforementioned tutor, according to the Vault at Pfaff's[1], an archive of New York City's artistic bohemians of the time, housed at Lehigh University, Bethlehem, Pennsylvania, which depicted him thusly:

"[He] delighted in studies and books, with now and

[1] As noted in the Caveat, this archive is faulty in spots, although the above information is not in dispute with regard to this writer's research.

then time taken for occasional verses, to be written and printed in the Poet's Corner of the Portsmouth Journal.

"Dialect tempered with slang is an admirable medium of communication between persons who have nothing to say and persons who would not care for anything properly said," the young bohemian maintained.

Aldrich's first volume of poetry, "The Bells: a Collection of Chimes . . ." was published by the firm of Derby & Jackson in 1854[1] . According to Charles E. Samuels, in his Aldrich biography, L.C. Derby of the publishing firm, noted the poetry book was not a

---

[1] Some references list a later year. However, according to C. A. Hazlett, his younger contemporary by a dozen years or so, the book was reviewed by C. W. Brewster, editor of the Portsmouth Journal on October 28, 1854 when Aldrich was still 17 years old. William Winter in his memoir implies he himself received a review copy in 1854, and critiqued it favorably in the Boston Transcript where he was employed. In turn, Aldrich dedicated a poem to him, heralding their 52-year friendship. There are two versions as to how their first face-to-face meeting took place. One - by Winter - is that it occurred the following year when Aldrich unexpectedly arrived at the Transcript offices to present himself to him. This unannounced meeting however does not tally with Aldrich's summertime correspondence that same year in which he arranges what he himself indicates is a first face-to-face meeting with Winter at the Revere House in Boston.

financial loss - neither was it a great money-maker.

"The Ballad of Babie (later Baby) Bell," believed to have first appeared sometime in the first part of 1855 (but prior to August 15), was inspired by the death of a three-year-old daughter of his aunt and uncle, Caroline and Charles Frost, and became his first widespread success. According to his friend, William Winter, it enjoyed worldwide circulation. Ironic then that it was first published in the Journal of Commerce, an odd outlet given the subject matter.

In a letter to William Winter, with whom he corresponded for several months before actually meeting in 1855, Aldrich spoke of his little cousin as a "very dear" friend. "I longed for her. I missed a hand that used to touch my hair so gently!" he wrote[1].

---

[1] The letter, written to express how he came to love the work of Longfellow, is confusing. Aldrich implies that the child's death occurred when he was 12 or 13 in the house where he was born in Portsmouth. That, at best, is highly unlikely since he moved with his parents and maternal grandparents a block away to what became the family home when he was just six weeks old. His birthplace, the Captain John Laighton House, could of course, have also been the one-time home of the Charles Frosts, but there is no evidence to support that possibility. The name of the house of his birthplace itself is muddled, inasmuch the house was built circa 1795 and Laighton himself wasn't born until 1784 (and died

On January 5, 1856 he received a check for $25 from Putnam's Magazine for his piece, A Legend of Elsinore," acknowledging payment by letter two days later.

The next month, he submitted more work to that publication in a February 21 letter to Charles F. Briggs thusly: "If the editor of Putnam's Monthly will give these verses an early perusal, he will confer a favor on his obliged servant." Calling for an "early perusal" one might deduce an "early impertinence" on the part of the callow teenager, fed by the first blush of successful sales.

From 1857 to 1859, he unsuccessfully attempted to have his work accepted and published in The Atlantic Monthly. Finally, in 1860 the magazine agreed to publish "Pythagoras."

In accepting it, James Russell Lowell wrote: "I welcome you heartily to the Atlantic. When I receive so fine a poem as "Pythagoras," I don't think the check of Messrs. Ticknor and Fields [publishers] pays for it. I must add some thanks and appreciation."

In New York, Aldrich was a frequent contributor to The Knickerbocker, as well as the aforesaid Putnam's

---

in 1866). It may have been built by his father or been his own domicile for a lengthy period.

Monthly. He was also known to have contributed to Vanity Fair.

In 1861, he had "Pampinea and Other Poems," published. Later he tried to buy back all extant copies and destroy them. He did not succeed in totality, but allegedly haunted several second-hand bookstores and perused auction house catalogues vigorously to tract down the book.

These examples of his having second thoughts on what he wrote were by no means uncommon. A sampling of his unpublished letters as compiled by Paulo Warth Gick for a thesis provides substantial evidence.

On February 23, 1856, while still a teenager, he writes Frederick Swartout Cozzens, an author that he has "just retouched and rewritten 'Baby Bell' and made it 20 percent better," in an effort to get the publisher of the "Cyclopaedia of American Literature," to reconsider its inclusion in that auspicious sounding publication. According to Paulo Warth Gick a different work "The Blue-Bells of New England," was accepted in a supplemental edition of the tome and a brief sketch of Aldrich published along with it.

On October 21, 1856, just three weeks prior to his 20th birthday anniversary, he asked Cozzens his opinion of "pruning" another poem and correcting "some defective lines" in order to have Putnam's accept it.

Aldrich made a decision to leave his uncle's employ and, "taking the cumbersome ledgers in his arms and depositing them on his uncle's desk, he declared that henceforth his sole allegiance would be to the Muse." That decision was forced upon him by his uncle's ultimatum to choose business or literature. William Winter, whom he first met as a teenage admirer, pinpoints the time of his quitting to the spring of 1856, which would make it after his hiring as a New York Evening Mirror junior literary agent in 1855.

His uncle – apparently miscalculating his ultimatum - objected to his nephew leaving the commission house, but allowed him to continue living in his home. His bedchamber was a third floor rear hall room (traditionally the tiniest sleeping room of all), until Aldrich married in 1865 and moved to Boston.

Twelve years later, in a December 13, 1876 letter to W. D. Howells, whom he would eventually succeed as editor of The Atlantic Monthly, Aldrich wrote of the disastrous Brooklyn (New York) Theatre fire eight days previously during a performance of "The Two Orphans" in which approximately one third of the 900 people in attendance, died.

"My uncle and all his family were in that Brooklyn

Theatre, and got out alive. One of my cousins reached the lobby *and went back and got his cane* – three rows from the footlights!" he revealed.

That was inexcusably reckless especially since the fire had started backstage when a kerosene light came in contact with hanging scenery.

Charles Frost died on or about October 31, 1880. In a letter of that same date to Winter, Aldrich wrote: "I have just returned from watching at the deathbed of my uncle, Mr. Frost, a faithful, good friend of my boyhood, and am heavy-hearted."

According to Sarah K. Bolton, in her "Biography of American Authors," a 19th century publication, Aldrich by age 18 had already published some press articles.

He had also become known as a writer of graceful, sentimental and ironic verse and had gathered enough work at age 17 to make the aforementioned volume "The Bells." Not a single title from this volume appears in his collected works. That is not to say, however that these poems have not survived elsewhere.

Marshall S. Berdan in his profile of the writer, noted Aldrich composed the work on the backs of bills of lading, while still in the employ of his uncle. C. A. Hazlett, his contemporary, maintained he did the same with "The Ballad of Babie Bell" with an added fillip "while unloading a vessel in New York owned by his uncle."

In a letter from Saranac Lake, Aldrich showed once again how he could be - in today's vernacular - a "control freak." On December 19, 1903 he disclosed to James C. Young, a bibliophile, that another collector Francis Bartlett of Boston owns "a book of [my] poems of which only six copies were printed on special paper. **Five of these copies I destroyed**." Though Aldrich offers no reason for their destruction, it is probable that he found their contents puerile. Paulo Warth Gick, in his Aldrich thesis, believes it to be the book published in 1885 by Houghton, Mifflin, titled simply "The Poems of Thomas Bailey Aldrich."

During his lengthy stay at The Porcupine, his Saranac Lake home built while his son Charles was attempting to convalesce from tuberculosis, Aldrich wrote among other works a volume of short stories titled "A Sea Turn and Other Matters." More importantly perhaps was "The Ponkapog Papers," one of his relatively few works of largely non-fiction in which his anecdotes add significantly to the author's makeup.

While he often rewrote his work even in its final stages and in some instances after it reached a publisher, Aldrich was adamantly against an outsider fashioning it to suit his or her purpose, as anyone might expect a professional writer to react.

For example, annotating an October 24, 1904 letter from Carrie B. Vaughan of Brockton, Massachusetts to his publishers, Houghton, Mifflin and Company, he wrote: "I object to her using the poem as a whole or quoting extracts from it." The lady had wanted to use his "Spring in New England" poem but omit and/or change lines!

On June 7, 1865 he wrote The Atlantic Monthly that if it chose to publish any of his recently submitted sonnets "don't do so without allowing me to see a proof, as I have several corrections to make."

According to the September 1898 edition of "The Gentlewoman," Aldrich worked in his den, the "highest point under the eaves" where only "those nearest to him," were permitted. No servant was allowed to put the room in order. Though admitting "the place looks like a cyclone struck it, he knows what's there and where everything can be found," the publication wrote. When working "he does not like to be disturbed [and] often waits for a mood." He "frequently rewrites."

In an earlier time Aldrich noted "the monument of letters which has piled itself up on my desk during my absence," after spending the Christmas and New Year holidays in New York. The observation was made on January 9, 1881, while writing to J. B. Kenyon, manager of a lecture bureau.

Always image conscious, Aldrich in a December 15, 1891 letter (apparently to a publishing house seeking a photograph of his work environment) confesses: "My books are scattered all over the house, and I have no library. My workroom – as Mrs. Aldrich will tell you – is a shabby little den in the attic, which I would not under any circumstances have reproduced."

William Henry Bishop, in The Critic, the literary magazine, said Aldrich allowed nothing "to be printed of his unless it has undergone at least three drafts."

On April 5, 1893, he complained to Henry M. Alden, editor of Harper's Magazine, that he had not received a proof of his submitted work and found the situation an "unpardonable awkwardness."

There is much more corroborative evidence to such fastidiousness, especially in Aldrich's unpublished letters. His punctiliousness is perhaps at its peak in a November 7, 1893 letter to Charles E. Norton, a founder of The Nation, the literary weekly. The short letter is solely devoted to making sure Norton eliminates **a single period** in Aldrich's piece involving Nathanial Hawthorne!

In a November 19, 1891 letter to William Bliss Carman of The Independent he criticizes the small size of typeface in printing his Cradle Song poem.

"Don't you think that if the Independent were to print its verse in larger type or space it more, it would be an advantage?" he asks. "I have a feeling that poetry needs every sort attraction in order to catch the eye."

In 1873 he records in a letter that he has been offered and has come to expect a 5% royalty on the list price of his books sold.

In a rather audacious letter dated February 4, 1875 to Henry Mills Alden, managing editor of Harper's Magazine, he orchestrates what he wants done with his submission, dictating price and time constraints.

"If the enclosed poem [Paulo Warth Gick identifies it as 'In an Atelier'[1]] is not worth the price I have marked on the manuscript," he writes "will you have the goodness to return it to me?"

Aldrich then directs Alden that upon acceptance "you could put the verses into type at once, that I may correct the proof before I go away. I am going to Europe next

---

[1] A charming 80-line characterization of a portrait painter as he intersperses his directions to his model with musings about Dante, love and art.

month, to be absent until January 1876."

Before that planned trip and just 23 days after penning that earlier letter to Alden, he writes a second missive ostensibly embarrassed for receiving a check larger than anticipated.

"I have so uncomfortable a sense of being overpaid," he tells Alden and offers him a sonnet for no compensation. It may have been worth just that for no such poem of his appeared in Harper's within a reasonable period of that free offering.

This writer, propounding a theory that is purely speculative, suggests Alden was not a man to be told what to do. When Aldrich placed a precise figure on work submitted, Alden gave him a better one. Throwing Alden a "bone" with the free sonnet, the Harper's representative was not about to lunge after it.

When his poem about Oliver Wendell Holmes was printed in Harper's Magazine without his corrected proof, he made sure a corrected version was published in The Critic, on May 6, 1893. Apparently Harper's did not insist on exclusive rights under the circumstances.

Planning to spend about eight months abroad, his 1900 trip was cut short after three months when his sister-in-law suffered a serious illness at home. Lethargy appeared to have overtaken him, despite his concern for ready cash.

In a letter to a publication, he asked for the balance on accepted work while telling the editor "I'm full of all sorts of literary plans which I shall take the greatest pains not to carry out."

There's little doubt that Aldrich enjoyed traveling and traveling well, but it is highly unlikely that he was lacking in financial means or resources, certainly not to the extent of the imbroglio to which his friend Mark Twain had become inveigled.

Marshall S. Berdan, writing in Adirondack Life Online claims that none of Aldrich's major works was conceived or completed in his country house in upstate New York while spending long annual stretches to be by his tubercular son Charles and his son's family.

Though one could debate the definition of "major," in at least one instance, Aldrich wrote of his work from Saranac Lake on October 27, 1903 that his volume of essays "Ponkapog Papers," was to be published the following day. In the letter, he asserted the editor failed to publish "immediately" his manuscript "On Early Rising," as stipulated months before, and that Aldrich subsequently revised it for inclusion in his new book. As noted earlier his "Ponkapog Papers" offered much needed insight into his thinking.

"Of all the places in the world, this is the place in which to read," Ferris Greenslet quotes Aldrich as writing about Saranac Lake. "It snows nearly all the time in a sort of unconscious way. I never saw such contradictory, irresponsible weather. It isn't cold here for human beings when it is 20 degrees below zero. Everything else is, of course, frozen stiff. The solitude is something that you can cut with a knife."

However, Greenslet also indicates that Aldrich found beauty there too. Aldrich himself found bizarre humor, noting he was cultivating a non-traditional "pet," to wit: a giant icicle.

"I am cultivating one that is already four feet long. I am training it outside, you understand, on a north gable, but I am concerned for it if warmer weather ever comes," he wrote according to Benjamin Pomerance of Pittsburgh, New York, in his feature article titled "Home Sweet Home" for the Lake Champlain Weekly.

Pomerance reported that on December 25, 1903 Aldrich was pleased to see that his son Charles came downstairs and sat upright in his armchair "smiling upon the children as gifts were plucked for them from the magical branches" of the Christmas tree. Presumably the children were Charles' little daughter Lillian and her older half-brother and half-sister.

Dry Spells

What appears to be an onset of writer's block following a period of lethargy encouraged by his sound financial status, had overtaken Aldrich, less than three weeks after declaring he had no intention of taking on an assignment about John Keats, the poet. On June 8, 1895, he writes Robert U. Johnson: "I haven't a scrap of prose or a stitch of verse . . . I have begun to think, recently, that I shall never write anything more. The mood seems to have left me – for good."

Some six months later he confesses in still another letter to Johnson of The Century: "I have not done a line of verse these 14 months, and I begin seriously to think that 'Her Majesty the Muse' has left me for all time."

On December 13, 1897 he writes Johnson of still another dry spell, noting the last time he created a work (it was an ode) was eight months ago.

"I have ceased to lay myself open to criticism by ceasing to write verse," he tells Johnson. "Seriously though, I envy every man who comes out with verse. Writing . . . has frequently deserted me **for months** together. This time it seems to have gone for good."

How Finances Appear To Have Affected His Work Output

Incredibly, despite the Henry Lillie Pierce legacy of 1896, following a 1900 trip to Europe aborted by his wife's family member's illness at home, Aldrich told Robert U. Johnson, associate editor of The Century, a popular New York quarterly journal in a May 21 letter, "I've come back a financial wreck." He requested that Johnson ask the company's cashier to send him a check for $50, the balance due on his work in "The Leaves from a Note Book." Yet, though saddled with his alleged penuriousness, in that same letter he speaks frankly of not wanting to work.

Five years earlier he had shed crocodile tears, writing to Johnson on May 22, 1895: "I find to my dismay that I haven't spent all my income for the last 12 months. I shan't go to work until that is done."

More specifically he told Johnson that he intended to write nothing that could not later be gathered in book form. Aldrich made that declaration in rejecting Johnson's offer of penning a piece on John Keats, "as I should have nothing to go with it in a volume."

Negotiations Prior, During and After Tenure as The Atlantic Monthly Editor

Unless otherwise noted, information under the above sub-head is primarily attributed to "A History of The Atlantic Monthly," by Ellery Sedgwick.

Aldrich was a reactionary, but as a rule did not use his nine-year editorship (1881-1890) on The Atlantic Monthly which he assumed in 1881, as an outlet for that view. However, according to Sarah Bolton, one of his biographers, some of his work did appear in the magazine while he was editor.

He also published poems by 120 other poets, about a third of them were women.

While Aldrich was a romanticist and a classicist and personally did not care for the writing of Henry James, a naturalist, he wanted and managed to secure James' services as a contributing writer to The Atlantic Monthly. Although James, author of "Daisy Miller," "Portrait of a Lady," and "Washington Square," considered Aldrich a "fatuous" man with "mediocre" talent, he nevertheless submitted and had pieces published in the magazine under the aegis of Aldrich, who harbored a general distaste for naturalistic prose.

Among James' works appearing in the magazine was a serialized version of "The Aspern Papers," a novella about a publishing scoundrel, in 1888, and the less well known "The Princess Casamassima," serialized in The Atlantic Monthly in 1885-86 and published as a novel in 1886. The latter work moralizes that the rich have a responsibility to use their wealth toward some useful end. Hilton Kramer, writing in the New York Observer newspaper on June 24, 2002, described it as one of James' "most audacious novels . . . which dealt with the subject of political terrorism and its support by the radically chic upper classes."

Although the standard fee at The Atlantic Monthly was $6 to $10 a page, Henry James once received $1,000 presumably for one of his works as serialized. However for "The Princess Casamassima" he "backed down" to a former Atlantic Monthly rate of $15 a page or about $350 an installment, according to Ellery Sedgwick's book about the magazine. In 1886, The Atlantic Monthly circulation was more than 10,000. Mrs. Aldrich claims Bret Harte was offered $10,000 for one year to write whatever he chose to write for it. However, the Harte offer was prior to Aldrich's ascension to the editorship in 1881.

Aldrich himself was paid up to $500 a poem (from Harper's Monthly) and $75 a page for his prose (from Century Magazine). Contrast this with Louisa Mae Alcott, who was earning 50 cents a page under a pseudonym for her penny dreadfuls, prior, of course to having "Little Women" published.

Aldrich solicited General William Tecumseh Sherman, while the scourge of the South was living in St. Louis, Missouri, but the general declined his offer to submit an article[1] .

In an April 10, 1890 letter to William Bliss Carman of The Independent of New York Aldrich confides that "the magazines pay me at the rate of three dollars per line for verse, **counting titles and spaces as lines**." Aldrich instead offered Carman a special discounted rate.

Henry C. Vedder admired Aldrich's editorship. "It was his good fortune to bring before the public for the first time writers, in both verse and prose, of now established reputation, and others, who may have appeared in print before [but] made their present fame during his editorship," said Vedder in his book on

[1] Sherman's demurring letter found its way to Mrs. Aldrich's brick museum framed on a wall.

contemporary writers.

A calculated practice in today's artistic and literary world – the limited edition – was evident in a February 24, 1892 letter to Henry Churchill DeMille (The father of famed Hollywood director Cecil B. DeMille, according to Paulo Warth Gick). He denied DeMille's request for autographed copies of an unnamed poem, explaining "I am under an agreement not to make any more autograph copies [because] the multiplication of such copies would take away from whatever value might attach itself to the original."

That was in marked contrast to his salad days as an author. Penned when he was 26, is a one-sentence letter to a fan, the sole purpose of which was to provide his autograph.

In a February 4, 1900 letter to Robert U. Johnson, Aldrich purchased photographic negatives of Edwin Booth, his late dear friend, with the intention of having them copyrighted, for purposes of controlling their dissemination.

In 1885, Aldrich led an Atlantic Monthly submitter down gently in an October 13 letter, when he wrote: "Your 'September Violet,' finds me in the last end of the December Atlantic. I can do nothing with such an untimely flower but return it to the florist who raised it.

This I do with many thanks."

In 1889, he rejected a manuscript from Woodrow Wilson, who was then a graduate student at Johns Hopkins. Wilson did not make a fuss about the rejected manuscript. Aldrich also rejected a manuscript from Charles Eliot, president of Harvard, who did fuss.

Aldrich rejected "Shakespeare's Viola," by J. F. Morton, claiming it catered only to a swarm of half-starved paupers. Morton wrote him: "You retained the manuscript nearly seven weeks . . . You did not read it or even open the package. . . You are a vulgar, unblushing rascal and an impudent audacious liar . . . You ought to be publicly horse-whipped."

Rejecting a young author's short story, Aldrich said while there were "beautiful" things in it, and it was well written, it was patently not interesting. He then invited the young man to lunch and offered him some money to tide him over if he needed it.

Once, while rejecting poems submitted to The Atlantic Monthly by W. C. Wilkinson, of the University of Chicago, Aldrich offered the poetry professor the chance to review the work of another, which Wilkinson accepted.

"I am unable to find a place for your ode," he wrote another aspirant on October 13, 1884. According to

Paulo Warth Gick in his Aldrich thesis, "this is one of the hundreds" of rejection letters The Atlantic Monthly editor dispatched in his nine years serving in that position.

Charles W. Chesnutt (1858-1932), was born and died in Cleveland, Ohio, and became a reporter for Dow Jones & Co. in 1883, then the New York Mail & Express, and a daily columnist of Wall Street gossip. In 1887 he became a lawyer, was one of the first black American writers of fiction, and wrote in the vernacular. Chesnutt, who also established a stenography business, wrote a biography of Frederick Douglas.

He sold three short stories to Aldrich for The Atlantic Monthly: "The Goophered Grapevine," in 1887; then "Po Sandy," in 1888 and "Dave's Neckliss," (sic) in 1889. Chesnutt had a 20-year association with The Atlantic Monthly, whereas Aldrich was forced to resign in 1890, after nine years.

Chesnutt's "The Goophered Grapevine," is a fable about a slave owner who resorts to bewitching his grapevine, to protect the grapes from thieves and slaves. A new slave eats the grapes and finds that grapes and tendrils grow out of his head. His strength and youth wax and wane with the grape-growing season. His master sells him in the spring and buys him back in the fall when he looks about to die.

"Dave's Neckliss," (sic) concerns the harm done to blacks by slavery. In the story the title character, a black man, is forced by a white overseer to wear a ham around his neck, upon suspicion of stealing. The degradation leads Dave to lose all sense of identity and commit suicide.

In "Periodical Literature in Nineteenth-Century America," Chesnutt's style is described as one who uses black dialect as the language of a crafty individual who steers his employer to a desired view.

In that same book, its editors maintain, "Aldrich seems to have had no idea that he was publishing an African-American author." In the opinion of this writer, that position stretches credulity. On the contrary, it would appear that Aldrich, by that time, a much-published author with wide-ranging contacts in the world of literature, would have realized Chesnutt's ethnic origin, if not initially, then almost assuredly through a colleague who would have recognized the name. Chesnutt himself, writing in The Colophon, a book collectors' quarterly magazine in 1931 recalled the time when the first of his "conjure" stories was accepted for publication "by Thomas Bailey Aldrich, the genial auburn-haired poet who at that time presided over the editorial desk." Chesnutt found "my relations with him, for the short time they lasted, were most cordial and friendly."

Aldrich resigned his position in June 1890 after Horace Scudder, literary advisor and trade editor, patently refused to fill in for him anymore during what seemed to be his interminable (averaging three to four months) European vacations. When Scudder succeeded him as editor, Aldrich said his successor was "greater than Moses," explaining that Moses dried up the Red Sea once, while Scudder dried up the Atlantic "monthly". As this writer found over and over again, Aldrich contradicted himself. In a December 13, 1901 letter to Henry M. Alden he sadly refers to Scudder's impending death, and considers their "old friendship intact."

According to Paula Blanchard, writing in "Sarah Orne Jewett," there actually existed "a long rivalry between Scudder and Aldrich," and the latter's eventual replacement by the former occurred "amid bad feelings on both sides."

Sarah Orne Jewett of South Berwick, Maine with whom Aldrich began his association as Atlantic Monthly editor and then befriended, in a letter dated June 23, 1890, wrote to him and Mrs. Aldrich:

"I was so overwhelmed when I got word of the change in the 'Atlantic's' fortunes that I don't feel free to express myself even yet! But this I can say, that I am most grateful for and unforgetful of all the patience and kindness which my dear friend the editor has given me in these years that are past."

His Inconsistent Philosophy on Veracity in Writing

Aldrich, in a preface for a later (1894) edition of "The Story of a Bad Boy," claims he "invented next to nothing," which he felt should satisfy the 1,500 to 2,000 "insidious" letter queries addressed to him by those of whom (presumably his younger readers) he considered no better than "autograph hunters," desiring to know whether the book is true. This contention is in sharp contrast to his public admission of it as a highly fictionalized novel 20 years earlier.

As for his fans, indications are that even in his own celebrity he himself was an autograph hound of the first water. For example, he mounted letters from the famous in red moroccan leather-bound gilt-edged autograph books. Also why wasn't General Sherman's letter not in The Atlantic Monthly archives where it belonged instead of the Aldrich museum?

In "Ponkapog Papers," he writes: "**No man has ever yet succeeded in painting an honest portrait of himself in an autobiography, however sedulously** [diligently] **he may have set to work about it. In spite of his candid purpose, he omits necessary touches and adds superfluous ones . . . It is only the diarist who accomplishes the feat of self-portraiture.**"

Additionally, he writes: "**Facts are not necessarily valuable, and frequently they add nothing to fiction** . . . True art selects and paraphrases, but seldom gives a verbatim translation." As an example he notes that an "author carefully excludes from definitive collective writings what others dredge up when he is dead!"

This last statement of his may have been his rationale for trying to destroy copies of two books of his poetry. These are "A Nest of Sonnets," and "Pampinea and Other Poems."

After having "A Nest of Sonnets," published privately in 1856, he later sought to destroy every copy but one. From it at least one poem "Ghosts," survives but was revised twice. As to "Pampinea and Other

Poems," after it was published in 1861, he tried to buy back all outstanding copies and have them destroyed. He did not succeed completely in this endeavor.

Marcia Jacobson in her book, "Being a Boy Again - Autobiography and the American Boy Book," asserts that "The Story of a Bad Boy," which is set in "Rivermouth," his pseudonym for Portsmouth, is not the wholly factual account that Aldrich claimed it to be. She writes:

"His book is not an autobiography of childhood; it is written with only perfunctory reference to the author's adult life. It is also less faithful to biographical fact than Aldrich's remarks suggest."

The most damaging evidence is in Aldrich's own words written 20 years before his own assertion that he "invented next to nothing." Those incriminating words appear in a letter written January 17, 1874 to the editor of the Portsmouth Journal, and published January 24, 1874.

It was precipitated by what Aldrich defended as a totally fabricated narrative (save for an allusion to a single building) in "Prudence Palfrey," a novel also set in "Rivermouth," whose name he used as well in 1872 for the story "Rivermouth Romance," in The Atlantic Monthly, (later published in book form in 1877.). Upon publication, "Prudence Palfrey," concerning a dedicated minister made to resign by church members following a half-century of faithful service, had set off a firestorm of criticism from the local Portsmouth citizenry who apparently found analogies to their lives in it.

"Three quarters of the narrative was pure invention," he states about "The Story of a Bad Boy," in relation to his stance on "Prudence Palfrey, explaining, "I have availed myself of a license which has always been granted to writers of romance."

It would be well if one could accept that last quote on face value, but obviously Aldrich was wont to contradict himself when he felt it was expedient. Still C. A. Hazlett, a magazine writer with whom he corresponded maintained "The Story of a Bad Boy" had "many local allusions, in nearly all of which he was an active participant[1]."

In his January, 1870 review of "The Story of a Bad Boy," W.D. Howells, then assistant to the editor, mused about what is true.

---

[1] The book is discussed in greater detail in Chapter VII.

"There must be a great deal of fact mixed up with the feigning, but the author has the art which imbues all with the same quality, and will not let us tell one from the other," he said. As an example, Howells cited the character of Kitty Collins' husband. We know that she existed in real life as a member of the Bailey household, but who her husband really was is less certain.

"Of her sea-faring husband, we are not so sure . . . [he] seems too much like the sailors we have met in the forecastles of novels and theaters, though for all we know he may be a veritable person," Howells concluded.

There were conflicting views of another sort regarding another Aldrich novel. Ferris Greenslet, in his biography of Aldrich, maintained "Prudence Palfrey" had "met from the start with a gratifying reception," directly contradicting the uproar that prompted Aldrich's defense of it. Even the fawning Greenslet had to admit that the novel "will scarcely take a place in the first rank of American fiction."

His Short Stories and Other Works

When "Old Town by the Sea," Aldrich's history of Portsmouth, was published in 1893, it received glowing reviews, despite its liberal borrowing from previously published work he did not originate.

"This title was selected by [him] in 1874 for a contribution to Harper's Monthly and in 1883[1] it was published with additions in book form," explained his contemporary C.A. Hazlett in a 1915 magazine article for The Granite Monthly.

Aldrich's "A Struggle for Life," has elements of Edgar Allan Poe and O. Henry in it.

He once explained when crafting his short stories, he always wrote the last paragraph first, avoiding all digressions and side issues.

From his collection of short stories "Out of His Head and Other Stories," published in 1863, "Pere Antoine's Date Palm," survives but in a considerably revised condition.

He had published a serialized story, "Daisy's Necklace and What Became of It," for the Sunday Atlas.

---

[1] The quoted book publication date is premature by a decade.

While Aldrich did write the pessimistic poem, "The Shipman's Tale," he later regretted that he had written in that negative vein because he believed that the function of poetry was to encourage humanity, not to discourage it. How he reconciled this position with his writing "Unguarded Gates," or "The Jew's Gift," has not been recorded to this writer's knowledge.

"The Jew's Gift," is a scabrous, graphic description of an orthodox Jew dead in an iron cage suspended from a tree in the year 1200 AD. The victim of an abbot's decree, he is left to sway in the spring breeze that stirs his long white beard. One day a passerby is startled to find the corpse clean-shaven but the purported "miracle" is more prosaic and horrific. Birds had picked it clean to feather their nests!

Because Aldrich cherished tradition, he would not embrace Realism and Naturalism. By the time he became editor of The Atlantic Monthly in 1881, he was disinclined toward the sentimental romantic gentility of Taylor and Stedman, two of his New York friends. He pursued Classicism and preferred not to use literature to explore the deeper, more complicated issues. Since his passing, he has been neglected unfortunately by readers during most of the last century.

Aldrich's Plays

William Winter, who was a critic for the New York Tribune for several decades and a longtime friend, said Aldrich "earnestly wished to excel in the field of the drama." Winter himself had his own standards. According to Cornelia Otis Skinner when Helena Modjeska played the title role in "Camille," he was disturbed by the casting.

"Even as established an intellectual as the critic William Winter publicly deplored the fact that this exquisite artist (and a countess too, mind you!) should debase her art by playing a fallen woman," wrote Miss Skinner.

"Mercedes," a two-act play that Aldrich had published in 1883, was produced 10 years later on Broadway at Palmer's Theatre on May 1, 1893, starred Julia Arthur, and ran a week. Just before the opening Aldrich, who apparently had not bothered to try on his evening trousers prior to leaving home, found that they no longer fit. He was then reduced to wearing his salt-and-pepper travel trousers with his evening jacket.

He sat in his box with wraps hiding his ill-matched "suit". After the performance the audience shouted:

"Author! Author!" which was his cue to go on stage, but Aldrich refused to do so. Instead, he stood behind a chair in his box to acknowledge the audience's fervor.

"Perhaps it is the cool conservatism of Boston that restrained him," stated one critic in a subsequent published newspaper article, attempting to explain Aldrich's unorthodox behavior.

Herewith the highly melodramatic plot of "Mercedes":

A certain Captain Luvois has been ordered to attack the Spanish hamlet of Arguano with a detachment of French soldiers and slay all of its inhabitants, including his beloved Mercedes, her child and her grandmother. Believing to have been betrayed by her lover, Mercedes drinks wine on orders from the soldiers who suspect it to be poisonous. Mercedes has her child drink as well. The soldiers have their fill and die. Luvois arrives to find a dying Mercedes to whom he reconfirms his love. At play's end "the curtain falls on a stage strewed with corpses," concludes Henry C. Vedder in whose biography of Aldrich the description appears.

In order to attend the premiere which he deemed "a success beyond my hopes," Aldrich wrote his friend,

William Winter on April 18, 1893 that he delayed a trip to Chicago to do so. Writing from Milton, Massachusetts, he told Winter he had closed his house in preparation for the trip. A subsequent letter to Winter on May 11 also listed Milton as its origin, but why he wrote from there is unknown since his known domiciles were located elsewhere.

In 1904 the same year his twin son Charles died from tuberculosis, Aldrich was prevailed upon by Nance O'Neil, a leading actress of the day, to dramatize his narrative poem "Judith and Holofernes." With his writing at a virtual standstill, not having the heart to take pen in hand because of his grief, Aldrich was eventually cajoled to do so. The result was "Judith of Bethulia," a biblical tragedy in blank verse in four acts, six scenes, which proved to be a success when it opened at the Tremont Theatre in Boston on October 13, 1904, more than seven months after Charles' death. Subsequently opening December 5, 1904 at Daly's Theatre, New York, it failed to have a successful run there, closing December 19. Aldrich writes in a January 17, 1905 letter to Robert U. Johnson, of "divided opinions," among critics, and he himself admits that during its short run "excepting one or two occasions the piece was wretchedly acted in New York."

John D. Barry, writing a review in The Critic, may have been biased in part, since Aldrich, in that same letter disclosed that Miss O'Neil, who played the Jewess heroine title role, had declined an offer to appear in Barry's own play. In the review Barry called for the omission of two characters, (it had a cast of 16), an altering of the plot construction and – according to Aldrich – a "change [in] the entire character of Judith."

Aldrich wrote Johnson that in private conversation Barry suggested that Miss O'Neil's character, empowered by divine grace to accomplish many deeds, perform the decapitation scene in full view of the audience!

"I am sorry that The Critic printed this rubbish, but The Critic has long been unfriendly to me," said Aldrich, who once again displayed his selective memory. In 1884 that literary magazine published a readership poll listing him as the seventh greatest living American male author, four places ahead of Mark Twain.

In an earlier (December 10, 1904) letter to Johnson, Aldrich regretted Johnson's having attended the New York premiere.

I am pleased that you liked [it] but regret that you did not see the second performance.

Miss O'Neil was not at her best on that first night, the

minor characters botched the text, and the stage mismanagement was such as would have given a black eye to Hamlet of Denmark or Macbeth of Scotland," he wrote, terming the production "heavily" handicapped. Later, following the play's closing Aldrich concluded that it was not only opening night but "the stage management throughout was excretable."

"If you don't want to pass sleepless nights, don't ever write a play, particularly a tragedy," Aldrich concluded.

Decades earlier, in 1866, he had abandoned work on a play he was writing in his spare time for his dear friend, Edwin Booth. To date, no other information about it has been uncovered by this writer.

VI. LITERARY AND OTHER CIRCLES

Poetic standards in New York were said to be less stringent than in the Boston literary world of Henry Wadsworth Longfellow, James Russell Lowell, Oliver Wendell Holmes, Ralph Waldo Emerson and John Greenleaf Whittier. One senses however that Aldrich had met more than one of them in New York before relocating to Boston in 1865, and dined and/or corresponded with them.

Among his prominent friends in Manhattan and elsewhere were Charles Dickens, who visited Aldrich's Pinckney Street home in Boston in 1867; and such other literary figures such as Samuel Clemens/Mark Twain, Harriet Beecher Stowe, Bram Stoker and Bret Harte[1], whom he probably met in 1871 when Harte moved to New York from California. Nathanial Hawthorne, who died in 1864, had corresponded with Aldrich while the

---

[1] According to Mark Sammons, a Strawbery Banke researcher, it was in the winter of 1871-72 that the debt-ridden Harte invited himself to stay overnight at the Aldrich home in Boston following an honorary dinner.

latter was still residing in New York.

William Winter, who had moved from Boston to New York in the winter of 1859-60, though their friendship had begun about a half-dozen years earlier, likely held a special place in his heart since their adolescent days.

There were poets Walt Whitman (whose "friendship" might be more loosely interpreted), Celia Thaxter, Sarah Orne Jewett (whose actual first name was Theodora), and the sculptor Augustus St. Gaudens. There is a surviving Aldrich family address book, compiled or added to by Mrs. Aldrich following her husband's death in 1907. An example on which this conclusion is based in that Mrs. Grover Cleveland[1] is listed alone, presumably after her husband, the late president, died in 1908.

---

[1] In a note card dated December 17, 1896, Frances Folsom Cleveland as she signed it, apologized to Lilian Aldrich for her tardiness in responding to her missive, explaining the pressures of preparing for Christmas in the White House. Incidentally, among the dozens of pieces of correspondence this writer inspected at the Houghton Library, only this note card and one sheet of stationery from Phoebe Garnant appear to be of better grade. While allowing for their age, nevertheless one was struck by the poor quality of the writing papers upon which the Aldriches and other such notables took pen in hand.

It is reasonable to assume however that Aldrich himself had known and corresponded with many of the addressees. For example, in an 1891 letter he refers to the Reform Club of New York. It was formed in 1888 at the end of President Cleveland's first term which, according to Paulo Warth Gick in his Aldrich thesis, contributed significantly in the nomination and re-election of Cleveland's non-consecutive second term in 1892. Gick notes a large proportion among its thousands of members were non-residents of New York, such as Aldrich by that time.

Additional figures of prominence include not only those with whom Aldrich was known to have had social intercourse, but those listed in the address book:

Renown in the theatrical field was Reginald De Koven, composer of many Broadway operettas, whose "Oh, Promise Me," is a perennial wedding song favorite. There were among his best friends actors such as John Drew, uncle of the Barrymores; Otis Skinner and Edwin Booth who found the organization in his five-story home at 16 Gramercy Park, New York for which Aldrich had the privilege of naming it The Players[1],which opened in

[1] In a letter to Winter, Aldrich objected to his having listed it as "The Players **Club**."

the 1880s[1]. That building, which dates to the 1840s, was almost entirely rebuilt by Stanford White, famous architect of the day and an original member.

There were leading actresses, such as Maude Adams, who originated in New York the role of Peter Pan, and corresponded with Mrs. Aldrich, and Julia Marlowe, Shakespearean portrayer. While not friends per se, Aldrich also met the internationally acclaimed Sara Bernhardt. He was also known to have corresponded with Joseph Jefferson, the renowned actor. According to Maria Deering, independent Manhattan tour guide, whom this writer met on November 15, 2003, Booth created the club to encourage respectability for the acting profession. Women however were not admitted as members until 1989, more than 100 years later.

Lilian Aldrich's desire to influence matters remained steadfast throughout her life. In 1925 at age 84 she managed to cajole the acclaimed British actor George Arliss into accommodating her 57-year-old son Talbot at a presumably sold-out performance. Since Arliss had closed in a Broadway production of "Old English" five

---

[1] One reference states the year was 1885, another in January 1888 and still another December 31, 1888.

months earlier, that was the likely vehicle in which he was touring.

"Dear Lilian," Arliss wrote on November 11, 1925, "If the worst comes to the worst, Tal can come 'round and sit with the girls behind the scenes – & then I suppose the worst will come to the worst."

Famous for their philanthropy were John D. Rockefeller and Andrew Carnegie. Also listed in the Aldrich address book were the U.S. Secretary of War Elihu Root and Charles G. Dawes, later destined for the vice presidency. The cream of Philadelphia society – Drexel, Biddle and Wanamaker families – was also included.

In New York, Aldrich would frequent Pfaff's, beneath the sidewalk at 647 (or 653) Broadway near Bleeker Street in Greenwich Village. Though ill-ventilated beer cellar, it was quite colorful. John Steusbaugh in his "History of Greenwich," describes it as having a "vaulted subterranean atmosphere of a rathskeller, noted beer selection [and], excellent wine list." He seated regulars at small tables set with "real silver and china."

Charles Pfaff, the proprietor, kept a long table in the rear of the premises for the bohemian crowd; Aldrich undoubtedly among them. As a gathering place for journalists and other writers, owing its vogue –

according to one Internet report – to the associates of the Saturday Press, to which Aldrich was associated by age 22. Beginning in his late adolescence he continued to spend time there with his fellow bohemians and other artistic friends, among them Walt Whitman, who first came to Pfaff's in 1859, There was Ada Clare, the *nom de plume* of Jane McElhenney, a bohemian poetess and sketch writer with acting aspirations, who cut her hair short and smoked cigarettes.

Other included Bayard Taylor, poet; William Winter, critic; Launt Thompson, sculptor and Sol Eytinge, Jr., illustrator of Charles Dickens novels. Another frequenter of Pfaff's where male and female artistic and literary figures mingled uninhibited, was Fitz-Hugh Ludlow, editor of Vanity Fair, at that time a humor magazine, who wrote "Biography of a Hasheesh Eater," based on first-hand experiences. In fact the whole of the Vanity Fair staff would meet regularly at Pfaff's.

In 1853 Aldrich first encountered his combative duel-loving tempestuous friend Fitz-James (née Michael) O'Brien. Born in County Limerick, December 31, 1828, he was graduated from Dublin University and had arrived in New York in 1852. O'Brien had a reputation as a mercurial writer of fantasies and dream stories (note the earlier cited "The Sewing Bird") resulting in fluctuating income.

Doubtless inspired by all that camaraderie, Aldrich penned “At the Café,” a poem that appearing in the Saturday Press on December 24, 1859.

“No literary circle comparable with the bohemian group of that period, in ardor of genius, variety of character, and singularity of achievement, has since existed in New York, nor has any group of writers anywhere existent in our country has been so ignorantly and grossly misrepresented and maligned,” said Winter, who in his 1909 memoir tried to set the record straight as - whom he believed to be - the last living frequenter of that Pfaff circle. He said the establishment, whose German proprietor made excellent coffee, was the haunt of mostly young writers and artistes who were usually impecunious. The owner was most congenial and – according to Steusbaugh “allowed them to loiter over their beers and run tabs.”

One of Aldrich’s earliest letters was uncovered by Paulo Warth Gick in his thesis. It is dated August 27, 1855 when the budding writer was just 18; acting quite the sophisticate. It was dispatched to William Winter, another teenager, who – after reading Aldrich’s published work (“The Bells: a Collection of Chimes,” where it was published a year earlier) – initiated a correspondence with him. Aldrich obviously relished the attention. Writing from New York he chastised Winter for not responding to his last missive. In that same letter Aldrich arranged for a one-hour meeting with Winter at Revere House[1] in Boston, where he would stay when in town.

"I shall be, unfortunately, engaged after eight o'clock," he wrote, "but if you will come at seven we can spend an hour together."

The rendezvous was to take place August 31[2], and Aldrich expected to return to New York the following day, since, he explained further "my business will occupy only an hour."

The two youths apparently managed to down a dinner and champagne in short order at the relatively new hotel

---

[1] The building was demolished in 1919.

[2] The date as previously indicated does not tally with Winter's account of Aldrich having popped into his Boston Transcript office unexpectedly to introduce himself. While Winter does not mention a specific date for that surprise visit (he writes: "our first meeting . . . occurred in the autumn of 1855), it nevertheless conflicts with Aldrich's version of a first face-to-face meeting in the summer of that same year.

built in 1847 on Bowdoin Square.

A subsequent Revere House rendezvous on September 9 failed to materialize when Winter never arrived. In another letter to him from New York dated September 13, Aldrich succumbed to all sorts of suppositions:

"I was much disappointed at your non-appearance – deeply so inasmuch as I attributed it to your being disappointed in me. I am afraid you didn't like me very well. I was too gay and wild for you, perhaps," he speculated. "I had just spent some delicious hours – they seemed like seconds – with 'my queen'."

Although Aldrich does not mention the young lady by name, she may have been Alice Cary of whom he wrote Winter most rapturously two months later. It is known however that he had several flirtations in his youth, in Boston as well as New York, Portsmouth and elsewhere.

Though they may not have met up to that point: "never touched a hand or exchanged a glance," Aldrich felt that through their correspondence "we have looked into each other's hearts."

One should also note that Victorians of a certain class tended to write effusively to the point where modern readers might misconstrue their meanings. For example, in this same letter to Winter he writes: "My [first] meeting with you has not broken a link of my love for you."

On July 9, a month earlier, Aldrich, confined to a sick bed, responded to a letter from Winter thusly: "How sweet is the letter that comes to a sick-room, fresh from the hand of a very dear though unseen friend!"

In correspondence between Samuel Clemens (Mark Twain) and William Dean Howells, who preceded Aldrich as editor of The Atlantic Monthly, there were similar sentiments.

Howells wrote he would rather have Twain's praise than of any living man except Leo Tolstoy "but I do not love him as I love you." Twain in turn wrote that he loved Howells as well.

In his book "My Mark Twain," Howells said he, Aldrich and Twain would spend hours at arranged luncheons and dinners discussing everything under the proverbial sun. One time in a whimsical mood Twain – as quoted by Howells – offered a far-fetched plan:

"He had a magnificent scheme for touring the country with Aldrich and myself [sic], in a private car, with a cook of our own and every facility for living on the fat of the land. We should read [before the public] only four times a week in an entertainment that should not last more than an hour and a half. He would be the impresario, and would guarantee us others at least $75 dollars a day and pay every expense."

The idea was quickly dismissed since Howells and Aldrich "both abhorred public appearances."

In a September 30, 1855 letter to Winter, Aldrich wrote of his having attended three days earlier "the dinner given by New York Publishers to American Authors. It is well enough for them to give the poor dreamy devils something to eat now and then. Authors, before now, have been hungry enough to eat poison."

Aldrich's abiding friendship with Winter, who became a long-time critic for the New York Tribune (some 30 years), lasted for more than a half-century, from their teenage years to Aldrich's death. Although Edwin Booth, the famous Shakespearean actor, condescendingly dubbed him "Weeping Willy," his reputation was regarded as influential and incorruptible.

There seems to have been a chink in Winter's incorruptible armor, however. According to Cornelia Otis Skinner, in her book "Family Circle," Winter was retained the summer of 1888 by the martinet manager Augustin Daly as his "personal critic" to his London production of "The Taming of the Shrew". As a well-known critic, local papers were pleased to print any items he might care to send them, and these items were "of course in the nature of polite boosts" for the entrepreneur's visiting American company.

"Daly paid Winter's expenses and occasionally gave him a present, keeping it all on an elaborately non-business basis," wrote Miss Skinner. "The morality of a manager hiring his own private critic is for a more ethical judgment than mine to determine."

Winter, in his 1909 memoir wrote of Aldrich, "during the last 52 . . . years I had the privilege of his friendship, and, although our pathways were different, and we could not often meet, the affection between us, that began in our youth, never changed."

In the archives of the Houghton Library at Harvard there is extensive Aldrich correspondence with Edwin Booth and Marie Thérèse de Solins Blanc, who wrote under the *nom de plume* M. Th. Bentzon, and was Aldrich's translator of his works in French. Aldrich also corresponded with Richard Harding Davis and Edward Everett Hale, noted for "The Man without a Country."

Aldrich's introduction to Mme. de Solins Blanc came about as a pleasant surprise. A friend, Ralph Olmstead Keeler killed in December, 1873 en route to Cuba as correspondent for the New York Tribune, had forwarded to her the Aldrich sketch "Marjorie Daw" without the author's knowledge. According to Paulo Warth Gick, the lady translated the Keeler-submitted piece for the Revue de Deux Mondes, and prefaced it with a flattering introduction of Aldrich and the American tradition of short story writing.

In a letter to her dated January 16, 1874, Aldrich expresses great satisfaction with the translation. "There were passages . . . which had a charm and a happiness [in French] not found in the original," he wrote. Mme. De Solins went on to translate more of Aldrich's works over time.

When Aldrich left New York, despite having lived there for nearly 18 years (from age 4 to age 9, and from 16 to 28) and establishing himself within the literary circle of Greenwich Village, he said he was lucky to escape with his English intact, and forevermore eschewed the label "bohemian". He and his colleague, William Winter had a conversation about his stance, as recreated in Winter's memoir:

"'Do you mean,' he [Aldrich] asked me, 'to cast in your lot with ***those*** writers? Do you intend to remain with them?'"

"I answered 'yes'," Winter asserted.

Aldrich felt at the time of his relocation that the

quality of the literary circle in Boston was far superior to what existed in New York. William Winter demurred in his 1909 memoir saying at that time the New England city "does not hold undisputed and indisputable pre-eminence in literature and journalism [but] then it was – and rightly called – the Athens of America."

Nevertheless Aldrich's words were belied by his deeds. He was known to have made frequent visits to New York over the succeeding decades. According to Sarah Bolton, one of his biographers, in 1880 his New York friends gave him a reception at the prestigious Delmonico's restaurant "glad and proud of his fame and success."

"He seems to have been a man who made friends easily, and he had also the qualities that hold friends once made. How much he is respected and admired by his fellow craftsmen was shown clearly in the public dinner lately given him by New York men of letters, who vied with one another to do him fitting honor," wrote Henry C. Vedder in his book on contemporary writers.

"That these [New York] years had an important part in the making of the man it would be absurd to question. The point is that in his writing there is singularly little trace of his New York life," Vedder claimed.

As late as 1901 Aldrich wrote in a letter from his

home in Boston, "I greatly wish to run on to New York."

It is interesting to note that a New York Times critic, in reviewing his play "Judith of Bethulia," which had a successful run in Boston, but was unsuccessful in New York, expressed a kind of snobbism in reverse.

"This sort of thing does well in Boston," the unnamed critic wrote, as quoted by Paulo Warth Gick in his Aldrich thesis. "Boston is itself a thing of archaic attitudes, if not of dusky splendors. But it won't leaven the Broadway lump, nor, indeed, the loaf of any vital artistic community."

The Aldriches and Twain

Both Aldrich and Twain) (1835-1910) lost their fathers at age 12. Twain later joined a company of Southern sympathizers and enlisted in the Confederate Army as a lieutenant, but after two weeks service, he managed to get himself discharged. Aldrich had sought postings with the Union Armed Forces as noted in Chapter IV.

An error precipitated their first direct contact. In the journal Every Saturday, Aldrich had reprinted some rhymes attributed to Twain, characterizing them as a feeble imitation of Bret Harte.

On January 14, 1871, Twain reacted and wrote: "Will you please correct your misstatement?" asserting that the excerpts were not of his doing. Aldrich did print a correction and the two struck up a lifelong relationship.

Twain's Pranks

In March 1874, Twain invited the Aldriches to his then residence (the Hook Farm) in Hartford, Connecticut, (his own permanent home in that same city was under construction), where they stayed two nights. The first morning as they were dressing, he knocked on their bedroom door and said: "Aldrich, come out. I want to speak to you." When Aldrich emerged, Twain said to him: "Are you emulating the kangaroos, with hobnails in your shoes, or trying the jumping frog business?"

That was Twain's way of asserting the Aldriches were too noisy and the din gave his wife, Olivia – called Livy - Clemens, a splitting headache. The Aldriches finished dressing "on tiptoe" and went downstairs "slowly and softly" to breakfast where they apologized profusely and asked Mrs. Clemens about her headache.

"Headache? I have no headache and our bedroom is in another wing," she replied puzzled.

Ever the autograph hound (though he chastised approximately 2,000 of his presumably young readers of "The Story of a Bad Boy," as autograph hunters, claiming their asking how much of "Story" was true was merely an excuse to obtain his autograph); Aldrich "demanded" a photograph from Mark Twain, in December 1874, nearly four years after they had met. Returning to his home in Hartford, Connecticut, Twain put up 52 likenesses in as many envelopes, intending to send one a week for a year.

Concluding that would be too slow a process, he decided instead to send one every single morning for a week or two, addressed to: "His Grace of Ponkapog," Aldrich's home in what is now Canton, Massachusetts. Aldrich protested the excessive response and the mailing appeared to stop. Then on New Year's Day, no fewer than 20 mailings arrived. They consisted of photographs and prints of Twain, his house, his family - even his personal belongings!

In a letter to his own wife Olivia, Twain referred to Aldrich as "the marquis of Ponkapog". Aldrich was also dubbed by Sarah Orne Jewett as "The Duke of Ponkapog," or a "linnet,' a small songbird that experiences color changes. Miss Jewett's biographer,

Paula Blanchard, suggests "bantam rooster," as the more apt description of Aldrich, who could be ostentatious.

There is irony in the fact that he chastised hundreds of these presumably young readers of "The Story of a Bad Boy," as making literary inquiries when he felt they were merely autograph hunters, with the fact that he himself kept handsome gilt-edged autograph books bound in red moroccan leather.

In this writer's opinion, a good example is his soliciting General William T. Sherman, the "scourge of the South," ostensibly to submit an article to The Atlantic Monthly. On November 26, 1883, General Sherman, responding from his residence in St. Louis, Missouri, wrote a short negative reply, stating that "I propose to take life easy . . . . "

If in fact Aldrich truly sought a piece for his publication, without ulterior motive, then why isn't this letter with the general's signature in the archives of The Atlantic Monthly, rather than originally encased in glass and framed in the Aldrich brick museum?

In 1900 Twain published a book entitled "My Boyhood Dreams," in which he presented as "gospel" fantastic stories about Aldrich and other contemporaries of his.

"It had been his hope to be a horse-docktor (sic)," he

wrote of Aldrich. "He is old now; he has ceased to struggle and is only a poet. No one would risk a horse with him now."

After receiving Twain's manuscript, the editor polled Aldrich and the others cited who replied they could not possibly find errors in fact when there are no facts, and they allowed the piece to be published with that caveat.

Twain's reaction as addressed to the editor: "Do not worry about these former young people. They can write good literature, but when it comes to speaking the truth, they have not had my training."

When Twain learned what he termed a South Carolina "idiot" attorney-at-law dedicated his "garbage" book "Plantation and Other Poems," to W. D. Howells, he wrote the former Atlantic Monthly editor in 1884 that if "this literary louse" had instead "dedicated this diarrhea to Aldrich, I could just howl with delight, but the joke is lost on you – just about wasted."

Twain's View of Mrs. Aldrich:

"A strange and vanity-devoured, detestable woman! I do not believe I could ever learn to like her except on a raft at sea with no other provisions in sight," he said.

According to J. Dennis Robinson, writing on the

Internet under seacoastnh.com on January 26, 2000, Mrs. Aldrich wrote of "a number of joyous encounters" with the Twains, "in Boston, in New York and while traveling in Europe."

Twain however wrote: "I conceived an aversion for her the first time I ever saw her . . . and that aversion has remained with me ever since. She is one of those people who are effusively affectionate, and whose demonstrations disorder your stomach. You never believe in them; you always regard them as fictions, artificialities, with a selfish motive back of them. Aldrich was delightful company, but we never saw a great deal of him because we couldn't have him by himself."

Hypocrisy is not limited to those without wit, for in a letter on file at the Houghton Library in Harvard, dated September 16, 1905, Twain wrote Mrs. Aldrich from the resort town of Dublin, New Hampshire, a letter filled with humor and his usual wit! Presumably she took it on face value and held it in high enough regard to preserve it.

Edwin Booth

By way of background, Edwin and his brothers Junius and John Wilkes Booth had performed together, opening in William Shakespeare's "Julius Caesar" at the Winter

Garden Theatre in New York on November 25, 1864, the Friday following Thanksgiving, before a crowd of 3,000. A critic noted that the acting of John Wilkes, who played Marc Antony, was the weakest among the Booth siblings.[1] Still the future assassin had managed to find other work on the legitimate stage, including tackling the formidable title role in the Bard's "Hamlet." It is ironic that on the same day of their joint theatrical appearance the three brothers were witness to a city-wide plot. Confederate sympathizers attempted to burn down New York by torching 19 hotels and other public buildings. Fortunately for the city, their bungling resulted in relatively little adverse effect.

Edwin Booth, famed as a Shakespearean actor, introduced Lilian Woodman to Thomas Bailey Aldrich, and served as best man at their wedding. They remained friends and he would occasionally dine with them.

The night of the assassination of President Abraham Lincoln, on April 14, 1865, in Ford's Theatre, Washington, D.C., Edwin Booth was performing in "The

---

[1] Edwin played the part of Marcus Brutus and Junius was Cassius. The one-night performance was a benefit to pay for a statue of Shakespeare erected in New York's Central Park, according to the League of American Theatres and Producers website.

Iron Chest," and "Don Caesar de Bazan," in a theater in Boston.

Twelve days after the assassination John Wilkes Booth was mortally wounded at Garrett's tobacco barn, near Bowling Green, Virginia, set afire by his pursuers.

Edwin Booth's career as a result was at a standstill. He received death threats and warnings that his house in New York City would be set aflame and the name of Booth "wiped off the map." Doubtless, his fair-weather friends were abandoning him. Thomas Bailey Aldrich, then 28, remained steadfast however. Still unmarried, Aldrich waited for his return from Boston with some loyal friends to greet him in his Gramercy Park home. He then moved in with Edwin Booth and lived with him in that New York residence until the crises subsided.

Aldrich and his fiancée Lilian were said to have attended the conspiracy trial of those eight persons implicated in the assassination in May 1865 in Washington, D.C.

Edwin Booth's first wife, Mary Devlin "whom he worshipped" according to Cornelia Otis Skinner, writing in "Family Circle," a biography of her actor-father, had died in February 1863 after less than three years of marriage.

"The accumulation of personal tribulation that had

dogged his life – his father's insanity, his brother Wilkes' crime that had shaken the nation, the death of [Mary] whose deathbed he had failed to come because he'd been so befuddled with drink he'd not understood the telegram until it was too late, his miserable existence with his second wife, Mary McVicker, a psychopathic (whom he married June 7, 1869) – all this had taken a toll of his sensitive endurance," Miss Skinner concluded.

In a letter to William Winter, mutual friend with Aldrich, the Shakespearean actor asked the critic: "Why do you not look at this miserable little life as I do?" Booth added he expected the cure for his emotional ills to come from "dear old Doctor Death."

During one episode in Booth's dressing room, Aldrich saw the actor's African-American valet prepare a glass of spirits for Booth. Aldrich intercepted it, opened a window, and threw its contents out.

William H. Rideing, in a reminiscence of Aldrich, published by Putnam's Magazine in 1910, notes that among the author's "dearest friends" was an "illustrious actor," an obvious allusion to Booth.

He said Aldrich saved the actor "from himself in long periods of depression, walking, riding and rowing with him during the day, and accompanying him to the theater at night in order to protect him from a gnawing and disastrous appetite."

In a letter to William Winter, the critic and longtime friend, dated May 11, 1893. Aldrich wrote he had caught a cold upon returning from New York for a farewell visit to a failing Edwin Booth.

"He did not know me until the instant I touched his hand, and then he smiled and said 'Tom Aldrich!' Immediately his mind was gone again, and he turned vacant eyes upon me," wrote Aldrich. Booth died at The Players, his home in Gramercy Park, Manhattan, just weeks later on June 7.

Aldrich, who had served as an honorary pall bearer at Booth's internment, wrote in a June 10, 1893 letter to Winter: "if there had not been a crowd of people, I would have buried my face in the greensward and wept, as men may not do, and women may."

Rideing credits Aldrich's patience and cheerfulness with the ultimate recovery of the "Prince of Players," who, while swearing he would never act again when disgraced by his assassin brother, returned to the stage January 3, 1866 as Hamlet, at the Winter Garden, to a New York audience's ovation. A practical aspect of his comeback was an improved income sorely needed.

Henry L. Pierce

The Honorable Henry Lillie Pierce, former mayor of Boston and congressman, who died without issue following a party on December 17, 1896,[1] left Aldrich $250,000, and $100,000 each to his twin sons, plus land at Ponkapog, an old Indian reservation, among other legacies. Aldrich himself had been living in that area off and on since 1874, and spent his final years at the Beacon Hill home in Boston. Samuel Clemens/Mark Twain claimed Pierce had a seaside cottage built for the couple and that Mrs. Aldrich had the politician at her beck and call "at considerable expense to his purse."

Pierce made the bulk of his fortune in cocoa, first working in the cocoa factory of his uncle, Walter Baker, and then leasing it after his uncle and his uncle's partner died. Baker's Cocoa became the leader in the field under his aegis.

---

[1] Greenslet, in his Aldrich biography, recounted the circumstance, which differ somewhat from the above version. Pierce was a houseguest in the Aldrich home at 59 Mt. Vernon Street, Boston, when felled by a paralyzing stroke rendering him speechless. He remained in residence until his death. Although Greenslet has him stricken in December 1896 he lists Pierce's death as 1897.

According to Aldrich biographer Charles E. Samuels since Pierce's will left a considerable fortune to Aldrich, he and his wife were able to travel extensively in Europe and around the world. It should be noted however that Aldrich's earliest known European trip was in 1875 and Pierce did not die until 1896, or 21 years later. Pierce's portrait, painted in 1895 by Joseph Florentin Léon Bonnat, was donated to the Museum of Fine Arts, Boston by Aldrich's twin sons.

He and Aldrich held opposing views, though perhaps they never aired them to each other. For example, Pierce fought against the Know-Nothings movement at the height of its power, while Aldrich espoused its views insofar as restricting immigration to benefit Anglo-Saxons was concerned. Wendell Phillips, radical abolitionist and son of the first mayor of Boston[1], said of Pierce if Diogenes had come to Boston "he would find his honest man in the mayor's chair." It is ironic that Aldrich was opposed to virtually all of Phillips' views as well, while courting Phillips' ward, Phoebe Garnant.

---

[1] Though first settled by Europeans in 1630, Boston did not have a mayoral form of government until 1822

Harriet Beecher Stowe

"I should like to make you and Mrs. Aldrich a little visit; the personality of your wife strongly attracts me," so said Harriet Beecher Stowe in inviting herself to what Lilian described as the "rose cottage" in the fishing village where the Aldrich's summer home was located. Mrs. Stowe was due to arrive the very next day, possibly in the year of 1871. (This writer was unable to pinpoint the exact date.)

Mrs. Aldrich was beside herself and when Mrs. Stowe arrived by train, much the worse for wear, she was offered a cooling claret. She was so overcome by the wine that she dropped off in a stupor on a sofa exposing her underclothes beneath the hoops of her skirt.

Fearing that Mr. Aldrich might arrive with an unexpected male guest as he was wont to do, Mrs. Aldrich attempted to cover her gently, but as she placed the coverlet upon her, Mrs. Stowe suddenly roused and uttered: "I won't be any properer than I have a mind to be. Let me sleep!"

Annie Fields, wife of James T. Fields, Atlantic Monthly editor from 1861-71 who died in 1881, presented an even more vivid view of Mrs. Stowe as a house guest. Mrs. Fields wrote in her journal she found the authoress of the seminal "Uncle Tom's Cabin," a sloppy eater dropping crumbs willy- nilly, yet a fine storyteller who rested her feet on the fireplace fender".

Oliver Wendell Holmes

Aldrich visited a dying friend - a doctor - intending to stay 15 minutes. He stayed three hours.

"I went there rather depressed, but I returned home leavened with his good spirits," he wrote, not mentioning the friend by name. According to Paulo Warth Gick in his Aldrich thesis, this friend was Oliver Wendell Holmes, who was in his mid-80s when he died October 7, 1894. Gick cites the Aldrich work "Leaves from a Note Book," as the identifying source. It had been Holmes of course to whom Aldrich sought literary advice 31 years earlier with his "Poems, with Portrait" collection.

VII. "THE STORY OF A BAD BOY"

"The Story of a Bad Boy," written in 1868 was at first serialized in Our Young Folks, a monthly magazine in 12 installments January through December 1869. It was then put into book form before the final magazine installments in the fall of 1869, although this first edition was actually dated 1870. One should note that the story was published a year after Louisa Mae Alcott's "Little Women," but several years before Mark Twain's "The Adventures of Tom Sawyer," which was published in 1876, and "The Adventures of Huckleberry Finn," in 1883. Also, "Bad Boy" went into 46 additional printings in the next 27 years until 1897. Several printings have been published in the ensuing years to date. One "Bad Boy" illustrator was A. B. (Arthur Burdett) Frost, a Philadelphia native, who also illustrated Twain's "Tom Sawyer." Though he bears the same last name as Aldrich's Uncle Charles Frost, no blood relationship has been uncovered.

Alison Lurie, in the June 24, 2004 edition of the New York Review, writes of "The Good Bad Boy," in literature and regards Aldrich's work as creating that classic character.

"This figure made his first important appearance in Thomas Bailey Aldrich's 'Story of a Bad Boy' (1869). Aldrich's hero, who was based on his own childhood self, is bad only in contrast to his priggish schoolmates, who lack a sense of enterprise and fun. He and his friends skip school and have adventures, but they do not go very far," Alison Lurie contends.

There have been Dutch, French, German, Swedish, Italian, Spanish, and Vietnamese[1] translations of this and other works. Aldrich was surprised to find a copy of "The Story of a Bad Boy," in his riverboat cabin while touring Imperial Russia.

In it he creates the character of Great Aunt Abigail, perhaps in real life a composite of his maternal grandmother, who did not die until 1861 and some spinster sister of his maternal grandmother or grandfather, who may well have been invited to take over household management (but not chores) upon the grandmother's demise, since the grandfather lived in the

---

[1] This writer was privileged to conduct a specially-arranged tour in 2017 of Aldrich haunts in Portsmouth for the Vietnam native translator.

house an additional nine years, dying in 1870.

Aldrich makes fun of Abigail's hot drops and notes that upon her death 87 empty phials are found in her bonnet box. In reality hot drops contained up to 20 % alcohol and laudanum, an early name for opium. In truth, one is more apt to view the Victorian maiden aunt with limited resources as less a subject of derision than pity.

The episode detailing his thieving and burning of a stagecoach for a midnight Fourth of July bonfire, happened all right – but not to the author. C.S. Gurney, writing about it in 1902 states unequivocally that Aldrich "**was not** a participant." This fact was re-confirmed by C.A. Hazlett, Aldrich's contemporary.

"The ex-mayor William H. Sise told me that Aldrich was not one of the bad boys who burned the coach," Hazlett wrote in a March 1915 article for The Granite Monthly.

Merging Gurney's version with that of Raymond A. Brighton, in "They Came to Fish," plus other accounts, it appears the incident occurred Sunday night July 4, 1847. William H. Sise was one of two ringleaders (the other was likely William H. Thompson) who resented a ban on bonfires by the town's selectmen mindful of the impending arrival of President James K. Polk on

Monday, the day after Independence Day[1].

An early visitor to the Thomas Bailey Aldrich Museum complex was Samuel H. Scott, 71. a private secretary of the commandant of the Soldiers and Sailors Home at Bath, New York, who said he figured in "The Story of a Bad Boy" bonfire episode on the Parade (the area now known as Vaughn Mall off Congress Street).

Scott, in a published account, said he was one of the party involved in the revelry. He said the stagecoach - believed to have been used in the 1700s for the scheduled weekly round-trip run from Portsmouth to Boston via

---

[1] While Brighton places the President in Portsmouth July 4, the July 13, 1847 edition of the New Hampshire Gazette states Polk's approximately three-hour long visit took place on Monday, July 5. Newspaper accounts of the day relate that the President was treated with proper decorum befitting his office, which makes it even more puzzling as to why Portsmouth's selectmen issued a ban on certain traditional celebrations, including fireworks. Yet on June 26, the Portsmouth Journal noted evening fireworks were to be scheduled for the July 5 celebration. Despite extensive efforts, this writer has uncovered no rationale for the ban. "He was received amidst the discharge of artillery," the Gazette related the day following Polk's visit, indicating that official ceremonial gunfire was not covered by that ban. One account has it as a 29-gun salute by the Portsmouth Artillery.

Ipswitch or Newburyport, Massachusetts - was taken from the Pleasant Street (near Washington Street) storehouse of Leonard Cotton, a local real estate magnate, to be torched . Another reference maintains the youths stole what was known as the Plow Boy stagecoach on the property of Hill & Safford, carriage makers, whose shop was at Market Square and High Street. Their misdeed was the climax to a night of mischief during which they refreshed themselves at the nearby confectioner's shop of Benjamin Whitcomb, at Fleet and State Streets.

In another publication, the Boston-Transcript, a reporter wrote of an encounter with Samuel Kingsley on the Paradc in Portsmouth, who said he too was present at the 1847 illegal bonfire.

"One boy, Samuel Spinney, from Christian Shore (a Portsmouth neighborhood) – a good deal of a daredevil – climbed into the coach when it had begun to burn. He sat on the seat and hollered: 'All aboard for Rowley!' Then he scrambled out - mighty quick!"

Sise went on to serve as Portsmouth's mayor (1878-1881), marking the occasion annually by eating ice cream in that same shop every July 3 for some reason, even during his term of office.

Decades later, Thompson, who became connected with the Kearsage Mills, arranged to have a stagecoach delivered from Boston to Mayor Sise's house at 2 a.m. on July 4, 1879. It too was then set afire.

Another famous episode in "The Story of a Bad Boy," is about a fort at the top of a hill where the Southenders boys would bombard the Northenders with snowballs. There is speculation that the site was Rundlett's Mountain, now part of Broad Street, a hilly section of town, or Slater's Hill, a section of State Street. The Southenders were those who lived in the area of Puddle Dock, centered upon a tidal salt marsh emanating from the Piscataway River. Most of the marsh was filled in by 1904 after shipping had declined as a major industry. For some unexplainable reason, Tom Bailey, the boy in the book is a Northender, but Aldrich himself was actually a Southender.

Perhaps the truth may never be known regarding the book's most poignant chapter. It is the one in which Tom Bailey's chum Binny Wallace drowns at sea. Binny leaves their river mouth encampment on "Sandpeep," an islet, to retrieve some lemons from their little rowboat which somehow breaks from its mooring and drifts into the open sea. Aldrich describes Sandpeep as "the last of the islands in the harbor," diamond shaped, with one shore facing the river and another the sea. In reality, the best fit to that description is Wood Island, but it is shaped more like a nugget than diamond in this 21st century. A perusal of the several Portsmouth newspapers of the day to confirm the drowning of a youth would require examination of microfilm (hardly the best, clear reproduction process) for at least a three-year period, 1849-52.

The realization that a number of Aldrich's contemporary and post-contemporary authors have published his biographical data based on "The Story of a Bad Boy," which, of course is fictional, is especially disturbing to this writer. Sarah K. Bolton, in her "Famous American Authors" is one who confuses fact with fiction and Henry C. Vedder, in his "American Writers of Today," published in 1894 and again in 1910, is another. Both however provide insights in other areas. It is his boyhood where these and other authors are apt to miss the mark. For example, because Aldrich does not refer to the years he lived in New York from ages four to nine in his novel, neither does Vedder. The implication is that the Aldrich family went directly from Portsmouth to New Orleans, which is simply not the case.

VIII. CRITICS ON ALDRICH'S WRITING

"Pampinea and Other Poems," published in 1861 by Rudd & Carlton Publishing Company, has as a sort of sub-title behind the cover of the volume, the words: "Poems of a Year." Taking his cue from that phrase, one unnamed critic described the book of poetry as "poems of a yearling."

It was not a great success and Aldrich eventually attempted to buy and destroy every copy he discovered in auction catalogues. The number cited is 25. Ironically, included in this volume is "Piscataqua River," apparently one of several poems devoted to the river of his youth. Henry Wadsworth Longfellow said this particular poem was the best in that book.

"The river will always be more beautiful for that song," said Longfellow who wrote Aldrich of his admiration for some of his work, including "The Curse of True Love Never Did Run Smooth," described as an Arabic love story poem, published when Aldrich was 21.

"The poem is very charming, full of color and

perfume as a rose. I congratulate you on your success," Longfellow wrote to Aldrich, inviting him when "passing through Boston," to visit him in Cambridge.

"It would give me great pleasure to make your personal acquaintance and to assure you of the interest I take in your career," he said in the letter quoted in the Greenslet biography.

Aldrich must have felt euphoric to receive such a missive from the man he hoped would have been his pedagogue had he been able to enroll at Harvard College.

Henry C. Vedder, a biographer, lauded his poetry:

"His workmanship approaches perfections [because] there has been no lack of the cutting and polishing," said Vedder, qualifying his conclusion by adding "he is a carver of exquisite cameos, not a sculpture of great statues."

Vedder felt Aldrich's long narrative poem "Judith and Holofernes"[1] was "conceived in the spirit of Milton and composed in the spirit of Keats." William Dean Howells, his immediate predecessor on The Atlantic Monthly, thought it "too Tennysonian." In a *billet-doux*

---

1 It became the basis for his Broadway play "Judith of Bethulia".

to his fiancée Lilian – addressing her as "*muchachita*" or little girl – Aldrich refers to her having the manuscript in hand. However, in the missive on file at the Houghton Library in Harvard, there is no indication he sought her input regarding the long narrative poem, presumably prior to its publication.

"While you are struggling through the poem you cannot help having the winter's wraith (don't mistake that for wrath) resting on your bosom and following your eyes from line to line. I hope you will like this poem – though it is in praise of another woman! I consider you a nice one to be jealous. What if I corresponded with a couple of *vivandieres* [*bon vivants*?] in the briny of the Potomac! Well, you couldn't, in the course of nature, love me as well as you do now," he wrote in one of the most romantic of his letters thus far uncovered. "If you only know how much delight a line from you would give me now, you would sit right down in front of that mottled green inkstand … and pen me an affectionate little note."

Aldrich continued to have doubts about his work. In a January 13, 1894 letter to Frank D. Sherman he discloses that upon perusing his sonnets he became "amazed at the badness of some of them." Subsequently he rewrote 24 of them and then apparently discarded two from that stack.

"When the [resulting] 22 sonnets are printed in the definitive collection of my verse, they will not disgrace us all, I hope," he said.

On another occasion and in a different context James Russell Lowell liked "Pythagoras," and called it a "fine poem."

Aldrich also received praise from Nathanial Hawthorne, John Greenleaf Whittier and Oliver Wendell Holmes.

After sending Holmes his "Poems, with Portrait," a collection published in New York in 1863, he received a frank critique from the man polled readers of The Critic were to deem the greatest living American male author in 1884. Holmes characterized "When the Sultan Goes to Ispahan," as "espiegle [mischievous], lively, poetical." On the other hand, he considered "The Lunch" as "a little Keatsy."

He wrote Aldrich: "You love the fragrance of certain words so well that you are in danger of making nosegays when you should write poems."

At its most damning, Holmes letter described some of Aldrich's choice of words as "inadmissible cockneyisms."

Holmes pointed out that ordinarily he responds with "vague generalities" to presentation copies, and making an exception in his case, he would expect Aldrich to accept his criticisms "kindly, for they are really complimentary."

That same collected edition of Aldrich's poems won commendation from Nathanial Hawthorne.

Poetess Sarah Orne Jewell commented in correspondence to Aldrich about "Shaw's Folly," one of his stories thusly: "The distinction between sentiment and sentimentality is a question of character …I love the way you have written that story. There's a realism seen from the humorous point of view: the trouble with most realism is that it isn't seen from any point of view at all, and so its shadows fall in every direction and it fails of being art."

It's apparent that Aldrich was in the habit of sending presentation copies of his works to established authors. Hawthorne wrote that he found his copy from Aldrich contained poems "rich, sweet and magnetic."

From Walt Whitman, regarding Aldrich's first slim volume of poetry, "The Bells," he told the then young author: "Yes, Tom, I like your tinkles, I like them very well." The inference from the wording of the quote is that it was solicited.

In William Winter's memoir the response of Whitman, who was 17 years older than Aldrich, was patently self-serving.

"Nothing could have denoted more distinctly, both complacent egotism and ill-breeding," wrote Winter, who asserted that Whitman "contrived to inspire Aldrich with a permanent aversion."

He related that the incident occurred in a milieu in which "the company was numerous, and the talk was about poetry." Winter, who did not have a high regard for Whitman to begin with had labeled the latter's "Leaves of Grass"[1] an "odoriferous classic." He patently was not enthralled by Whitman's bohemian reputation.

"He did not impress me as anything other than what he was, a commonplace, uncouth, and sometimes obnoxiously coarse writer, trying to be original by using a formless style, and celebrating the proletarians who make the world almost uninhabitable by their vulgarity," wrote Winter. He said that Whitman at that time affected a style of shirt and jacket that "made no secret of his

---

[1] Garrison Keiler in a National Public Radio broadcast July 4, 2006 said the slim tome, comprised of 12 poems and a preface, was unveiled July 4, 1855. Whitman had had it published privately. Steusbaugh in his "History of Greenwich Village," cites 1854 as the first edition with an output of 800 copies. He stated the only positive reviews were ghost-written by Whitman himself.

brawny anatomy and his hirsute chest."

Yet, D.H. Lawrence, in his "Studies in Classic American Literature," first published in 1923, numbered "Leaves of Grass," among his list of significant books, and it continues to hold a distinctive place among Victorian works.

Opinions differed as to Aldrich's place. E. C. Stedman, whom Aldrich had known in New York, and who later served as one of his honorary pallbearers, said Aldrich's existence had been one of "absolute success," according to Caroline Ticknor, writing in "Glimpses of Authors."

On the other hand, Henry James thought Aldrich displayed "mediocre" talent, and was "fatuous.".

Henry C. Vedder, writing in "American Writers of Today," devotes an entire chapter to Aldrich and though he falls into the trap of other contemporary authors by assuming the early boyhood accounts in "The Story of a Bad Boy" (which eliminates his years from 1841-46) and has the family going directly from Portsmouth to New Orleans, had several astute remarks pertaining to his character.

"As a mark of sounder taste, that in later editions of ["Ballad of Babie Bell"] Mr. Aldrich has dropped the affected spelling that originally spelled this poem, and now we have the "Ballad of Baby Bell," Vedder wrote.

"It was a few affectations like this (sic), and a somewhat dandified style of portrait published with some of his earlier works, that made many people look on Mr. Aldrich for a long time as a literary 'Miss Nancy'. They were slow in giving him credit for the real virile power that these writings show," he said.

Thomas Beer, writing in "The Mauve Decade," uncovered one of the most scabrous descriptions of Aldrich in an anonymous verse that dubbed him "the beau of Boston town," and denigrated his efforts thusly:

"What though, like a lady's waist/All his line[s] are overlaced?/What though, from a shallow brain/Smooth inanities he strain?/In his emptiness content/He achieves his ten percent ..."

William S. Braithwaite editor of the annual "Anthology of Magazine Verse", in a posthumous sonnet on Aldrich, called him "the Wondersmith of vocables."

Samuel Clemens/Mark Twain, in speaking about Aldrich to Robert Louis Stevenson, said:

"Aldrich has never had his peer for prompt and pithy and witty and humourous sayings. None has equaled him; certainly none has surpassed him, in the felicity of phrasing with which he clothed these children of his fancy. Aldrich is always brilliant; he can't help it; he is a fire-opal set round with rose diamonds; when he is not speaking you know that his dainty fancies are twinkling and glimmering around in him; when he speaks the diamonds flash. Yes, he is always brilliant, he will always be brilliant; he will be brilliant in hell - you will see."

"I hope not," Stevenson responded, apparently not anxious to join Aldrich in Hades.

"Well, you will, and he will dim even those ruddy fires and look like a transfigured Adonis backed against a pink sunset."

On another occasion, Twain waxed effusively as well:

"Aldrich was always witty, always brilliant," said Twain, who likened that wit to Charles Maurice de Talleyrand-Périgord, the French statesman.

Additionally, he said "when it came time to making fun of a folly, a silliness, a windy pretense, a wild absurdity, Aldrich the brilliant, Aldrich the sarcastic,

Aldrich the ironical, Aldrich the merciless, was a master."

Twain and Aldrich were said to have argued over who was the first to create a bad boy character. The Twain piece "Story of the Bad Little Boy" as retrieved from the Internet however is dated 1875, six years after Aldrich's tome was published, although there appears to have been two earlier versions, both predating "The Story of a Bad Boy." According to Mark Sammons, a museum researcher, in a draft dated July 8, 1998, it was first written in December, 1865 and revised and re-issued in 1867 and finally in 1875. In Twain's short-short story the bad boy's villainous deeds go unpunished; the good boy gets the switch for the bad boy's theft. It reaches an absurd climax when the bad boy marries, takes an axe to his family and becomes a legislator!

On a personal level, Twain indicated he would like to have spent more time with Aldrich (he once inscribed a novel to him: "From your only friend") but circumstances would not permit. "Mrs. Aldrich would scalp me if I tried to beguile him," he said.

All of these accolades by Twain and yet, in 1908, the year of the dedication of the Aldrich Memorial Museum on whose board of directors he had agreed to serve, the author wrote a number of less than laudatory comments about Aldrich (and others at various times) *in petto*, directing that the Aldrich account not be published for 75 years. However, instead of 1983, some of it was published in 1922, just 12 years after Twain died but five years **before** Mrs. Aldrich had expired, and to which she had access as a published work.

The indication in a footnote (p. 292) in the 1940 edition of "Mark Twain in Eruption," is that this account of the memorial service did not make the 1922 edition. Apparently, there are still parts of the Aldrich account that have not been published to date. According to Bernard DeVoto, editor of the 1940 edition, "certain other passages, which were not only biased but vindictive, would cause pain to living persons." He wrote he conferred with the Twain Estate which allowed publication upon prudent editing. DeVoto said as a result, he felt he needed to omit "relevant parts of the text. The reader is denied several pages of personalities that are full of flavor..."

Presumably, there exists a repository containing the entire unexpurgated account. As inflammatory as the 1940 published account is, one can only imagine what has been omitted.

Twain said the reason he wanted what he was writing in 1908 suppressed for three-quarters of a century, is because "I want to talk without embarrassment and speak with freedom - freedom, comfort, appetite, relish."

There's little doubt that Twain – his talent notwithstanding – was an embittered man. In his autobiography he admits to having been bankrupt in Europe "and was finding it difficult to make both ends meet. Mrs. Aldrich entertained Mrs. Clemens and me by exploiting in a large way various vanities of hers in the presence of Aldrich and poor[1] old [Henry] Pierce – they apparently approving."

Twain described in detail her adamant position in insisting that only deluxe and not mere first-class sailing accommodations be made available to her on a trip to Japan. She succeeded in obtaining one of only two $750 suites on the promenade deck.

"Think of it!" wrote Twain. "Why damnation! She had been a pauper all her life, but here she was strutting around on those lofty stilts."

Twain said Mrs. Aldrich stocked her husband's boyhood home "with odds and ends that once belonged to the child Tom Aldrich, and to the schoolboy Tom Aldrich, and to the old poet Tom Aldrich."

---

[1] In this context Twain calls the very rich Pierce "poor" as synonymous with victimized.

He found the justification for the memorial museum doubtful.

"Aldrich was never widely known; his books never attained to a wide circulation; his prose was diffuse, self-conscious and barren of distinction in the matter of style; his fame as a writer of prose is not considerable; his fame as a writer of verse is also very limited, but such as it is it is a matter to be proud of," he asserted.

Twain maintained the verse that engenders pride is not based upon Aldrich's output as a whole, but upon half a dozen small poems "which are not surpassed in our language for exquisite grace and beauty and finish." Unfortunately in this context, he does not enumerate them.

He suggested that if the Aldrich museum were in Boston or New York City it would attract no more than one visitor a month. The inference is that its Portsmouth location would attract fewer. In actuality in its last year of operation as an independent museum, prior to its being turned over to the Strawbery Banke Museum, it had attracted 300 visitors, but ten times or possibly more (sources vary) in its first short - June 30-September 26, 1908 - season.

William Dean Howells, Aldrich's predecessor as editor of The Atlantic Monthly, was repelled by

Aldrich's capacity for self-appreciation and dismissed him after his death as being "out of the world rather than out of my world." He also criticized Aldrich for not addressing issues of the day in his poetry and for not writing in a naturalistic style. Strange, since Howells felt compelled to be at the museum dedication service. He, of course, had been known to travel in the same social circles as Aldrich and in 1902 wrote him praising "The Story of a Bad Boy."

"You have no idea how your personality peoples Portsmouth for me with the young Aldrich. We are boys together," he said.

Thirty-two years earlier, Howells, then assistant to James T. Fields, editor of The Atlantic Monthly, in his review of the Aldrich work, lauded it as precedent-setting.

"No one else seems to have thought of telling the story of a boy's life, with so great desire to show that a boy's life is, and so little purpose of teaching what it should be, certainly no one else has thought of doing this for the life of an American boy," he wrote. "On the whole we think the chapter which tells of [Binny Wallace's] loss is the best in the book."

In 1866 a critic named "Torrini"[1] whom Aldrich considered "quarrelsome and irresponsible" and arriving with "foreign grievances," in reviewing "The Poems of Thomas Bailey Aldrich," criticized the poet as seldom attempting to deal with "any feature or incident of our national life; for this might have demanded a realistic treatment foreign to his genius."

According to Justin Kaplan in "Mr. Clemens and Mr. Twain," he (Twain) "found nothing to admire in 'The Story of a Bad Boy'."

That same year (1866), Nathanial Hawthorne's wife, Sophia, wrote Aldrich, waxing rhapsodic about his revised story, "Pere Antoine's Date-Palm," and said her late husband who died in 1864 had "demanded" to see the remainder of the prose piece after sampling a portion.

"I thank Heaven for gifting you with this most ethereal delicacy of genius, for all our sakes," wrote Mrs.

---

[1] Apparently a *nom de plume* or pseudonym since library research has uncovered no such critic. Torrini, however, is the name of a controversial character in Aldrich's novel "Stillwater Tragedy," though it was not published at that time but 14 years later. It would not surprise this writer that he named the checkered character after this adversary for spite. Incidentally, some critics regard "Stillwater" as anti-union, though Patricia Kane, a Strawbery Banke historic interpreter, read it in 2004 and preferred to term its theme "pro-management."

Hawthorne in her closing.

Helen Keller inscribed a book to Aldrich with these words: "From a bad girl to a bad boy."

Post World War I reaction to Victorianism led to Aldrich no longer being read with the same acclaim. This was due largely to H. L. Mencken of the Baltimore Sun and his ilk who felt that for the most part - he sometimes excepted Mark Twain - Victorian writers were sappy sentimentalists and not worth reading.

The most devastating influence contributing to the decline of Aldrich's literary reputation was the widespread post-World War I reaction to certain societal aspects of 19th Century Victorianism. Under Mencken and others, New England Puritanism and gentility in manner were held up to ridicule. Aldrich himself, relatively early in his career, aimed for individuality of style, stating that "a man must depend wholly upon himself – the less of anybody else he carries with him the farther he will go."

Mencken's bombastic essay "Puritanism, a Literary Force," although discredited by some, was taken with high seriousness by so-called liberated intellects of the 1920s, following its publication in 1917.

"A novel or a play is judged . . . almost entirely by its orthodoxy of doctrine, its platitudiousness, its usefulness as a moral tract," he asserted. Mencken labeled John Greenleaf Whittier and James Russell Lowell "second raters" and found the writings of Henry Wadsworth Longfellow "pious gurglings". As for Sarah Orne Jewett, whose poems Aldrich welcomed in the pages of The Atlantic Monthly, Mencken lumped her writings among those perused as "an experience that is almost terrible."

C. Hartley Grattan, writing in the American Mercury, declared the since-deceased Aldrich "never had anything to say . . . Never looked at life directly. . .
[And wrote] escape poetry of the most vapid sort."

Grattan felt that Aldrich's much-admired poem "Spring in New England," was nothing more than "word-dropping of a pious sentimentality for the war victims buried in the far away South."

He also felt that even his widely-acclaimed "The Story of a Bad Boy," could not compare with Mark Twain's "Huckleberry Finn."

William H. Rideing, in his 1910 memoir, "Glimpses of T. B. Aldrich," considered him "old fashioned" in many ways.

"Perhaps he was too fastidious for his age, and at all events whatever others were doing he persistently lived up to an ideal which appraised moral responsibility at no less a value than the symmetry and orderliness which he strove for and achieved in his own literary art," Rideing wrote. "Stories of mean things and squalid situations repelled him even when they were well told."

He said Aldrich "more than deplored the slap-dash methods which pass without censure in many of the popular books of the day: the ungraceful and untrained plungings of that new school of writers which violates every classic tradition and formula of the literary art, and flings its work at the reader like so many entrails."

Ferris Greenslet, in his biography of Aldrich, said as early as his New York bohemian period, "he soon became known as the wielder of a rapier that no man cared to trifle with."

In 1884, The Critic, a New York-based literary magazine, conducted a readership poll to name the greatest living American male authors with a view toward including them in a possible American Academy. In order of their popularity, Aldrich came in seventh place with Twain in eleventh place. The list:

1.Oliver Wendell Holmes, **2.** James Russell Lowell,

3. John Greenleaf Whittier, **4.** George Bancroft[1], **5.** William Dean Howells, **6.** George William Curtis, **7.** Thomas Bailey Aldrich, **8.** Bret Harte, **9.** George W. Cable, **10.** Henry James, **11.** Mark Twain, **12.** Walt Whitman, **13.** John Burroughs.

However, 15 years later a similar readership poll was conducted in the American edition of Literature, among its magazine readers to determine their choice of ten living writers also for induction into an American Academy. Although the running order during the three-month poll presumably kept changing, at its approximate mid-point Twain came in second, this time outranking Aldrich, who was fourth. The list:

1. Howells, **2.** Twain, **3.** John Fiske, **4.** Aldrich, **5.** James, **6.** Frank R. Stockton, **7.** Harte, **8.** H. Weir Mitchell. **9.** Charles D. Warner, **10.** Cable.

In one of Aldrich's last available letters, written just three weeks before he was stricken with an illness leading to his death two months hence, he retained his

---

[1] Born in Massachusetts in 1800, he wrote 10-volume history of the United States.

razor-sharp tongue. Noting someone described his "Kriss Kringle," a poem about a snowflake-sprinkling Santa as "quite like a stocking." Aldrich surmised the commentator to be "some phenomenally dull person."

Winter, his longtime friend had kind words for Aldrich and his body of work:

"We first met in 1855 and from that time till his death, March 19, 1907, our cordial friendship remained unbroken. We had maintained an active correspondence for several months before we became personally acquainted – he being then resident in New York and I in Cambridge, Massachusetts," wrote Winter in his 1909 memoir.

"His published writings exhibit his soul, as the writings of a poet always do," said Winter noting that in his youth Aldrich was attracted to oriental themes. "The child was father to the man; and the man, to the end of his days was the apostle of beauty and the incarnation of kindness. His character rested upon a basis of prudence, and in the conduct of life he was conventional."

Winter found him to possess "a happy faculty of quick rejoinder and quizzical remark."

He described the death of Aldrich's son Charles as age 35 as the one cruel blow from which Aldrich never recovered.

"Some of his short stories are exquisite in their felicitous finished utterance of his fancy, sentiment and humor," opined Winter. "His poetry is supreme in the element of grace, and he maintained precisely the right attitude toward it and toward criticism of it."

A widow wrote Aldrich her little daughter died and asked if he could possibly send her about a dozen lines from a poem he wrote on the death of an infant girl (presumably the "Ballad of Baby Bell"). Aldrich was so moved by the widow's letter, he transcribed the entire poem of about 100 lines for her.

Two months later, Aldrich spotted that same missive for sale in a second-hand bookshop.

This writer has attempted elsewhere in this book, but particularly in this chapter, to illustrate how Aldrich's peers would often contradict themselves in their opinions of him, depending upon the time and circumstances. That is not to say Aldrich himself did not contribute to the seesawing palaver within his social circles. As the next chapter will show, hypocrisy abounds!

IX. ALDRICH'S OPINIONS OF OTHER WRITERS

In a letter dated December 30, 1876 to Bayard Taylor, regarding publication of his latest (unspecified) book, Aldrich noted that of the 30 notices afforded it, "25 of them are simply illiterate."

"Mark Twain's humor is not to be classed with the fragile plants; it has serious root striking deep down into rich earth, and I think it will go on flowering indefinitely," Aldrich said, of the writer who – despite political correctness – endures to this day.

Emily Dickinson (1830-1886), except for seven anonymous verses, had her poems unpublished during her lifetime. Poems found after her death were published for the first time from 1890-1936. Presumably, Aldrich had two years to read her attributed verse before describing her as second rate in January 1892. He writes disparagingly of her work, stating that only isolated phrases are truly poetic. He said she showed only "intermittent flashes of imagination."

Aldrich found her rhymes impossible and her poems' significance too involved.

As for poets John Keats and Percy Bysshe Shelley, he is totally dismissive. "Keats delights me not, nor Shelley," he writes in a letter dated May 22, 1895.

When it suited him he could be obsequiously humble. For example, on December 4, 1868 Aldrich, in acknowledging James Russell Lowell's gift of an autographed copy of "Under the Willows," wrote:

"I sit here, chuckling to think how the perplexed collector will stare at my name on the fly-leaf and wonder who the deuce I was to receive such coin from the mint itself."

Aldrich attempted to avoid Oscar Wilde. During one stay of the Irish playwright in Boston, Aldrich declined all invitations to luncheons, dinners and receptions so as not to meet him. Later that year (which year?) they met on a train, apparently by accident.

According to Richard Ellman in his book "Oscar Wilde," Aldrich was not alone in avoiding the controversial Irishman.

"There were some writers, such as [Edmund] Clarence Stedman, who made a point of not accepting invitations to parties that Wilde might attend," said Ellman. He noted that Stedman in turn wrote to Aldrich that Boston "this Philistine town is making a fool of itself over Oscar Wilde [who] has brought hundreds of letters of introduction."

Besides boycotts Wilde faced hecklers[1]. At his January 31, 1882 opening, 60 Harvard students had reserved the first two rows of the Boston Music Hall, keeping them vacant until just before his appearance.

Then the five dozen collegians marched into the auditorium *en masse* wearing knee breeches and black stockings, each waving a lily or a sunflower, as they were led by a leader who dropped listlessly with limp wrist and vacant eye into his seat. Tipped off in advance, Wilde chose not to wear his signature costume.

"I see about me certain signs of an aesthetic movement," he announced, "but I can assure them that they are no more than caricatures. As I look around me, I am impelled [to acclaim] save me from my disciples!"

In retaliation, the students applauded heartily whenever Wilde took a sip from a glass of water.

Sometime in the early fall of 1892, Henry Irving, the

---

[1] This account combines the version in Ellman's book as well as that of Barbara Belford's "Oscar Wilde, a Certain Genius."

Shakespearean actor, threw an after-theater supper on the stage of the Lyceum Theatre, Boston. Ellen Terry, a star attraction and the "Divine Sarah" Bernhardt were among the glitterati, as were Aldrich and Wilde, accompanied by his wife, Constance. Wilde, that particular evening, happened to be "conventionally" dressed, which must have surprised the Portsmouth native.

"Mr. Wilde had dropped his masquerade [and] discarded his unwise and foolish attitude," recounted Mrs. Aldrich, of the soirée. In an October 3, 1892 letter to William Winter, Aldrich in recounting the evening felt the need to comment on Miss Bernhardt's "unraveled hair." If Wilde did refrain from playing the poseur, it was a transient moment. In "The Wilde Album," written by his grandson, Merlin Holland (his family changed its name from "Wilde" after the public scandal; the trial over his active inversion) and published by Henry Holt & Co., New York 1998, his grandfather is quoted thusly:

"I have two secretaries, one to write my autograph and answer the hundreds of letters that come begging for it. Another whose hair is brown to send locks of his own hair to the young ladies who write asking for mine; he is rapidly becoming bald."

It appears that Aldrich would have preferred to - in the vernacular - "cut him dead." On January 20, 1882, while editor-in-chief of The Atlantic Monthly, he wrote his friend Edmund C. Stedman that he thought of imitating the Irish playwright's style, "but have decided not to do so. Nothing cuts a showman or a literary clown like no notice at all." The piece would have been placed in the magazine's Contributors Club, which featured light banter. Given such strong feeling against Wilde, it is difficult to accept Ellman's claim in his book that Mrs. Aldrich was in attendance at his funeral. Wilde, born October 16, 1854 had died November 30, 1900 and was initially buried at Bagneux Cemetery in France[1]. It is highly unlikely she did attend, as the Aldriches had to cut short in April, 1900, their proposed eight-month European vacation which began in February. The reason was news of the serious illness of Mrs. Aldrich's sister in America.

This writer has been unable to uncover any evidence that Mrs. Aldrich (or her husband for that matter) returned to Europe in the late fall of that year. Ellman

---

[1] In 1909 his remains were moved to Père Lachise Cemetery in Paris.

depicts her following the coffin and has her counting the number of mourners - 14 – at the funeral service which took place in early December 1900.

Aldrich felt Henry James' realistic approach was not good literature. However, he was astute enough to know the value of a James piece in The Atlantic Monthly and while he was editor there managed to convince James to submit some work. Although James found Aldrich "fatuous with mediocre talent," he did not refuse the $1,000 offered him. Normal Atlantic Monthly rates were substantially less. "Monthly" in the magazine/s title was dropped in 2007 since publication was reduced to 10 issues a year. It has also relocated its facilities to Washington, D. C. and New York.

While Aldrich had foreseen the rise of Realism and Naturalism, his own artistic integrity would not permit him to change his subject matter or his style merely to satisfy current tastes.

Paulo Warth Gick, in his Aldrich thesis, discloses what he believes to be Aldrich's dislike of the work of James Whitcomb Riley.

In a June 5, 1896 letter to Robert U. Johnson, associate editor of The Century, Aldrich takes a dim view of Johnson's praise for his – Aldrich's - last submitted sonnet in remarking Riley could not have written a better one.

"I am thinking of sending back that $50," he tells Johnson. "[Since Riley] couldn't have written a better sonnet [your comparison] gives me a feeling of having been rather over-renumerated."

"Riley wrote much of his poetry in the 'Hoosier dialect,' a technique that was not acceptable according to Aldrich's standards of purity of language, form and style," Gick concludes.

Aldrich wrote E.C. Stedman on June 10, 1897 he found Ralph Waldo Emerson's "Bacchus," growing "finer day by day," and the writings of Alfred Lord Tennyson made him "a king of simplicity and beauty."

In that same letter, he said he found that the patriotic and "occasional" poems of John Greenleaf Whittier and Oliver Wendell Holmes have "already undergone great shrinkage."

One of his frankest criticisms uncovered was in a submission by William H. Bishop to him as editor of The Atlantic Monthly. On May 12, 1885, Aldrich wrote that the manuscript written in pencil no less, "is so carelessly prepared as to make very hard reading." Aldrich's professionalism is revealed in the fact that he does not simply make that blanket statement, but supports it in detail.

"Here and there you have put descriptive passages between quotation marks, and omitted them in the dialogues," he explained. "I everywhere found sentences that present themselves wrong and foremost and some that were meaningless because of this misconstruction."

To balance out his position, he said he liked the idea of the story to the extent he had submitted it to two other readers for their independent opinions.

"I have lain awake nights thinking over the matter, and can arrange it in no way but the way suggested," Aldrich concluded.

When S. Weir Mitchell sent him a limited edition copy of his "Hugh Wynne," he responded in a December 26, 1897 letter that it and the late Nathanial Hawthorne's "The Scarlet Letter," constituted "the two chief pieces of American fiction." The assertion seems patently overblown.

Celia Thaxter was renown for her salons on Appledore Island, part of the Isles of Shoals off the coast of the Maine-New Hampshire border, in which Aldrich was said to have been a participant, along with many other famous personages at one time or another such as Henry Wadsworth Longfellow, James Russell Lowell, Oliver Wendell Holmes, Ralph Waldo Emerson,

Nathanial Hawthorne, Sarah Orne Jewett, James Greenleaf Whittier, Samuel Clemens (Mark Twain) and Childe Hassam, the artist. Marshall S. Berdan, writing in Adirondack Life One Line, cites Lowell, Holmes, Emerson and Hawthorne, among the guests at Aldrich's home in Boston.

This writer has found limited evidence Aldrich set foot in his native city again, following his maternal grandfather's death there in 1870. One Aldrich letter dated April 5, 1872, discloses he was "down to old Portsmouth to pick up some of my native air" but fails to record the length of stay or any specific location. His grandfather's house had been sold two years earlier.

In her 1983 paper prepared for lecture, Marie Donahue said Aldrich "occasionally took the electric cars" to visit Sarah Orne Jewett in her South Berwick, Maine home. A telephone interview with Ms. Donahue on December 23, 2004 ascertained she was referring to electrified trolley cars.

According to O.R. Cummings in his introduction to Bulletin #1 of the New England Electric Railway Historical Society, Inc., dated December 30, 1964, one line found in 1901 and serving the greater Berwick area absorbed a previously constructed line serving the greater Portsmouth area in 1903. One may conclude therefore that Aldrich visited Miss Jewett via an electrified trolley car between the years 1901-1907.

Aldrich consenting to board such a conveyance is somewhat ironic, in view of the fact that he himself had once deplored the establishment of horse-drawn cars on Charles Street in Boston!

One may further conclude that even decades following the death of his maternal grandparents, he continued to visit the Portsmouth area. How frequently however, is another matter. As to Aldrich's actual presence at Celia Thaxter's famous salons on Appledore Island, there has been much talk, but a paucity of printed references come to light.

Marie Donahue, in her 1983 paper prepared for presentation at St. John's Church, Portsmouth, does depict one such salon scenario:

"Celia invited her guests to perform too. Visitors might hear William Mason, the boy prodigy who had toured Europe as a concert pianist, playing a Chopin prelude; or Julius Eichberg, the celebrated German violinist . . . watch Childe Hassam . . . painting [her] or her garden; [or] chat with Whittier, Hawthorne, Lowell, Howells, **Aldrich** and Sarah Jewett."

It is known that Mrs. Thaxter's friendship with the Aldriches was both social and professional. In 1880 at dinner in Rome with Aldrich and another friend, Elihu Vedder, an American ex-patriot painter, the trio discussed the spirit of life after death, inspiring Aldrich to pen these gothic lines on the spot:

Somewhere in desolate windswept space
In Twilight land – in No Man's land
Two hurrying shapes met face to face
And bade each other stand
"And who are you?" cried one, agape
Shuddering in the glooming light
"I know not," said the second shape
"I only died last night!"

Aldrich's poem prompted Vedder to do a pencil sketch at that same dinner of a pair of draped figures. Some time later Mrs. Thaxter asked Aldrich to copy his "wonderful dreadful poem" in dimensions compatible with placing it under Vedder's sketch for framing.

On October 4, 1881, all remained sweetness and light when Mrs. Thaxter penned a note to Mrs. Aldrich accompanying a bibelot:

"Will you accept this little milk jug which I have decorated with Shoals marigolds for you, and use it on your breakfast table to remind you of your friend [?]"

Although Mrs. Thaxter, Aldrich's own "old friend" had her poetry published in The Atlantic Monthly under his editorship, it was in July, 1885 that he last deigned to do so, when he published "Within and Without." She had been first published in that magazine as far back as a quarter-century in March of 1860, with her poem "Land-Locked".

By January 12, 1888, two-and-a-half years later, her relationship with him appears to have soured somewhat, when she wrote him in his continuing capacity as editor of The Atlantic Monthly:

"If you don't want this poem, kindly return it in the enclosed envelope and oblige," she wrote, adding a traditionally warm but - under the circumstances - suspect closing: "Yours always cordially, Celia Thaxter."

"The note suggests somewhat strained relations with her old friend," Rosamond Thaxter wrote in her grandmother's biography.

In this case his opinion of her writing may have changed. If Aldrich did purchase the poem it apparently was never used – a not uncommon practice then and now.

When it came to his appreciation of the talents of Sarah Orne Jewett, it was a different matter. Not having had a Jewett submission for a while, Aldrich wrote to her in rhyme:

Cute little spider down in Maine
(all the time we need her)
Spin some silvery webs again
To catch the flying reader

On another occasion Aldrich wrote: "whenever you give me one of your perfect little stories, the whole number seems in bloom!"

Little wonder with such adoration Miss Jewett would dub him her linnet bird.

Conversely, in an incredible admission in a letter to Miss Jewett, disclosed in her biography by Francis Otto Matthiesson, Aldrich "admitted his own stories had no *raison d'etre* other than to amuse."

In a February 3, 1894 letter to Robert U. Johnson, associate editor of The Century, he charges one of his works was essentially plagiarized by Bow Bells, a London-based magazine.

"[It] has stolen a novel of mine ["Prudence Palfrey," according to Paulo Warth Gick], changed the title, rechristened the characters and printed the thing as a serial. The Yankee Blade of this [presumably Boston] town copies it!'

Gick reveals that in the February 24, 1894 edition of The Critic, the New York-based literary magazine, the double-pirating was reported and that the Blade had reproduced the work from Bow Bells on the excuse that the British publication printed it without a byline, which – apparently at that time – allowed anonymous work to be lifted at will!

"His books have been pirated freely by those canny European publishers who have stolen both wisely and well," opined Henry C. Vedder, one of Aldrich's biographers.

The famed Greenwich Village haunt of his youth, Pfaff's Beer Cellar (or Cave as some called it), so active in the 1850s, had faded early in the next decade, "gradually deserted by the votaries of the quill and the brush, and the day of dreams was ended," wrote Winter in his memoir.

In 1880 Aldrich waxed nostalgic about that time when penning a letter to Winter:

"How they have all gone, the old familiar faces! What a crowd of ghosts people that narrow strip of old bohemian country through which we passed long ago!"

Poet and Portsmouth native Albert Laighton (1829-1887), a cousin to Celia Thaxter, was especially dear to Aldrich, as a youth.

"I would lay down [my life] to save his," he wrote his friend, William Winter on July 17, 1855, when he was 18 years old. "He writes very tender, beautiful verse."

Aldrich seemed determined to not only familiarize Winter with Laighton but to create a colloquy via an exchange of letters among the three of them.

Winter wrote that he and Laighton did become close friends and correspondents.

"His name was seldom in print and his writings are practically unknown," said Winter. "Laighton was not the bearer of a great poetical message, but he sang sweetly of love, confident faith and resignation."

Aldrich was said to be enamored of the work of Robert Herrick. According to Winter, he considered himself to be "the disciple of Herrick."

This writer has unearthed two literary figures bearing that name. One (1868-1938) was a novelist, who according to one encyclopedia was "part of a new generation of American realists." Since Aldrich was a classicist and romanticist, one would hardly expect him to follow in the path of that much younger writer. The other and more likely candidate (1591-1674) was an English poet, who – again according to an encyclopedia - is "generally considered the greatest of the cavalier poets." Interestingly this Herrick was a disciple of Ben Johnson and his lyrics are said to show considerable classical influence.

Aldrich blanched at certain continental non-fiction writing. "French novels with metaphysical or psychological prefaces are always certain to be particularly indecent," he asserted.

X. ALDRICH'S OTHER OPINIONS AND PREFERENCES

It is clear from this writer's point of view through years of research that Aldrich was contradictory in his views on diverse subjects on a number of occasions. He criticized New York, yet repeatedly revisited it even in old age. The Irish were the brunt of his jokes, but he once roomed with one and maintained a long friendship with another. He was even more scathing when speaking or writing about Jews, yet a Jewess was the heroine of his long narrative poem-turned-play and he numbered Bret Harte (Mrs. Aldrich noted Harte had "Hebrew blood") among his companions. He made fun of Catholic ritual, yet requested an audience with the Pope, managed to visit Rome during Holy Week, and witnessed the decennial Passion play in Oberammergau, Germany more than once! One could argue that Aldrich was prejudiced in the general (hence "Unguarded Gates," his misanthropic poem and his membership in the Immigration Restriction League, detailed later in this section) but not in the specific. One could also argue that he aimed his venomous barbs at certain targets for no reason other than to manifest the cleverness of his wit. Whatever the truth – and it might be even more complex than posited – many today would consider the label "bigot" not unjustified. Yet, during his nine years as editor-in-chief of The Atlantic Monthly, the evidence of his thorough professionalism when dealing with women, minorities and opposing literary styles is there for all researchers to see.

"Though I am not genuine Boston, I am Boston plated," he once declared.

He was considered vain in his dress and overall appearance. Aldrich himself admitted as much. In a letter to Bayard Taylor dated May 8, 1864, he likened his demeanor at that time to "an irreclaimable egoist".

On June 10, 1897 he wrote E. C. Stedman: "none of my photos does me any justice."

Samuel Clemens/Mark Twain said that Aldrich's vanity when "bunched together" with that of Stedman, a critic, matched his own.

Although he detested the Abraham Lincoln type of stovepipe hat, Aldrich, said Rideing, was once spotted wearing a new silk hat, while hesitating to enter the office of his colleagues.

"I am afraid they'll laugh at this," he explained.

During a trip to England, Aldrich, a Mayflower descendant, wrote to an Atlantic Monthly colleague he "associated so constantly with persons who don't do anything for a living that, on undressing at night, I have examined myself to see if I bore on my person any hitherto undiscerned birthmark in the shape of a court-of-arms."

He mounted the letters he received from famous people in leather-bound autograph books with gold lettering, as earlier noted. He had at least two book plates custom-tailored to his taste: one with his three-part name and his mark framing a plate with the mask of comedy at its center; the other with his name in old English lettering with the tiny figure of a bull as the cynosure.[1]

---

1 The plates and a letter dated April 29, 1886 from New York City are housed in the rare collections room at the Portsmouth Public Library. They were presented to the library by his son, Talbot "in memory of my father." In that letter, addressed to a man whose initials are J.T. S. (the handwriting clouds his last name), and another letter that same day to Frederick Swartout Cozzens, Aldrich discloses he has been retained as a reader for the firm of Derby & Jackson, which had published his first book of poetry "The Bells" several decades earlier. Since he was to hold his formidable position as editor of The Atlantic Monthly for several more years, the appearance of a conflict of interest would

Aldrich ordered all of his books bound in scarlet moroccan leather flat back gilt with trimmed gilt-topped edges. In a letter to Elbridge H. Goss on June 6, 1894, he criticized the quality of the paper on which Goss' biography of Paul Revere had been printed.

Preparing for an 11-month European vacation, he outlined his plans to Henry Mills Alden, Editor of Harper's Magazine in a February 4, 1875 letter, and asked: "Do you not envy me? I almost envy myself."

His snobbery was such that he withdrew from the National Institute of Arts and Letters because he said it "included everybody who was ready to pay the yearly dues, and gave one about the same distinction that one would get in a city directory." In a January 17, 1905 letter to Robert U. Johnson, Aldrich expresses satisfaction with its offshoot, the National Academy of Arts and Letters, established April 23, 1904, by retaining membership there. According to Paulo Warth Gick, in his Aldrich thesis, this academy was more exclusive, restricting its membership to 50 - Aldrich being among the first seven admitted.

He previously had resigned from the Tavern Club,

---

seem to be evident here.

complaining in a February 10, 1893 letter to H. W. Mabie that "a fellow couldn't eat his dinner there without . . . being called upon."

In an October 3, 1892 letter to William Winter, his longtime friend, he was critical of what he termed "the stupid strangers who make life a burden to me. Half of my waking hours are wasted on persons who have no business to write to me, and yet must . . . be treated courteously."

His anti-immigration stance is threaded through some of his prose and poetry, and he was inclined toward a reactionary view. One example of the latter trait is his opposition to change, even objecting to the introduction of horse-drawn cars on Charles Street in Boston, as previously mentioned. Writing to his longtime friend William Winter in 1884, he cited "the shortsighted, intolerant prohibitionists, the howling woman suffragists," and others, while conceding "they all mean well – confound them!"

As for the former, examples abound.

In 1883 Emma Lazarus (1849-1887), Jewish poetess, wrote "The New Colossus," which implored: "Give me your tired, your poor . . . the wretched refuse from your teeming shores. . . " In 1908 this poem was inscribed on a tablet at the pedestal of the Statue of Liberty.

In 1894, Aldrich wrote "Unguarded Gates," which is antithetical to the Lazarus piece. He himself termed his work "misanthropic," but felt it needed to be said. In it, he cites " . . . A wild, motley throng . . . Bringing with them unknown gods and rites [speaking] strange tongues . . . Accents of menace to our air." His poem appealed to the "white goddess" of liberty to "stay those who to thy sacred portals come to waste the gifts of freedom . . . lest from thy brow the clustered stars be torn and tramped in the dust."

Among the undesirables he cites are: "men from the Volga and the Tartar steppes, featureless figures of the Hoang-Ho, Malayan, Scythian, Teuton, Kelt and Slav," and ends by asking: "Is it well to leave the gates unguarded?"

Aldrich blamed increasing immigration for the dilution of the New England character.

On a steamer from Gibraltar to Tangier, Morocco, Aldrich spotted an Englishman with a bathtub on board. He said Arabs circled around it, not having any idea what it was, but suspected it might be some sort of newfangled armor or even a huge frying pan. He said the Jews knew full well what it was, despite never having used one!

Aldrich felt that each great town in the United States had its "Little Italy [district] but one dare not linger there after nightfall, since the chief industry of these exotic communities seems to be spaghetti and stilettos."

Surprisingly, in a July 15, 1899 letter written from The Crags, in Tenants Harbor, Maine, to Robert U. Johnson, Aldrich calls for treatment "with Christian decency a people who for the last 100 years have been fighting bravely for the right of self-government, a right that ought to appeal to Americans who once fought for the same thing and were less justified."

His reference is to the Filipino nationals, who now came under United States jurisdiction following the Spanish-American War, a war in which his son Talbot may have been an Army major.

According to "Periodical Literature in Nineteenth-Century America," Aldrich "was given to ethnic slurs masquerading as witticisms, in one instance placing more value on his dog, Trip, than on the Irish population of Boston."

While editor of The Atlantic Monthly, Aldrich did have a setter named Trip, who would fetch his slippers and present them to him. Sarah Bolton, the writer, had seen the dog in his office and found it a "beautiful" animal. She observed when the dog wanted to be walked it would climb up four flights of stairs, remove Aldrich's hat from a hatbox and lay it at his master's feet. When

Trip died, Aldrich was so embittered; he wrote that the dog showed "better manners and more intelligence than half the persons you meet . . . Why should he be dead and these other creatures exhausting the ozone?"

This reference to "creatures" is thus regarded as the Boston Irish.

Among the East Side slums of the Bowery in New York "stretches a malodorous little street wholly given over to long-bearded merchants of ready-made and second-hand clothing," wrote Aldrich. "The contents of the dingy shops seem to have revolted and rushed pell-mell out of doors and taken possession of the sidewalk."

Aldrich, in "Old Town by the Sea," said the immigration situation is such that he expects a "Chinese policeman with a sandalwood club and a rice paper handkerchief, patrolling . . . " in Portsmouth.

On February 12, 1870, the Portsmouth Journal re-published a letter from Aldrich, which had been sent to the Springfield (Massachusetts) Republican in response to its mistaken impression that the writer was of Irish descent.

"I do not forgive him for robbing me of my nationality," said Aldrich of the original newspaper article writer. "He cannot now, even if he were inclined, undo the mischief. Of all the journals that have copied his statement, probably not one in ten would reprint a retraction. Thus many a well-disposed person will go down to his grave with the impression that my real name is possibly, Ma**loon**ey . . ." The irony is that John Boyle O'Reilly, Irish novelist, poet and editor, was a good friend and drinking companion, who was banished from his native land for violent revolutionary sentiments. His life sentence was commuted to 20 years penal servitude in Australia, but according to the Catholic Encyclopedia he escaped in 1869, assisted by the captain of a New Bedford, Massachusetts whaler. He became editor of The Pilot, a Boston publication, the following year in 1870. In 1880 he was a co-founder of the St. Botolph Club in that same city.

As a married man, Aldrich labeled his own Irish cook (**not** his grandfather's cook) "the despot who reigns over our kitchen." He was a product of his time in which certain people of his caliber found persons of Irish birth or extraction objects of great dislike and distrust.

As previously noted he was considered an anti-unionist. "The Stillwater Tragedy" has been labeled an anti-labor novel, because of its pro-management sentiments and opposition to the general strike. It also fosters an anti-ethnic bias. Set in a stonecutting yard, the story concerns an Italian who organizes the laborers of northern European stock. Aldrich condemns the protagonist for trying to effect change.

A biographer, Henry C. Vedder believes it to be "his most ambitious prose work," citing his more complex characters.

"The moral element in the book, while wholesome in its intent, is vitiated by sentiment. There has been no treatment of the vexed 'labor question' in fiction that is not weakened by its sentimental tone," posited Vedder.

Aldrich was clearly fastidious in his creativity. It reached its pinnacle – as described in Chapter Five - when he penned a letter to The Nation to eliminate a single period on his previously submitted piece.

On Socializing:

William H. Rideing said "one could never be mistaken as to his likes and dislikes, for he was frankly outspoken whenever anything jarred him."

Yet, at a Massachusetts governor's birthday celebration for Harriet Beecher Stowe, he was downright inarticulate when pressed to address the gathering, according to Rideing.

"He was incurably shy among strangers, especially in

public gatherings of all kinds, and had a strong aversion to speech-making," Rideing explained, mitigating Aldrich's outspokenness, at least in that situation.

Aldrich himself admitted as much. In an October 31, 1887 letter to Robert U. Johnson, associate editor of Century Magazine, he declines an invitation to speak.

"A while ago I was induced to give a reading, with other authors, at the Boston Museum," he explained, noting the occasion was a money-raiser for the Longfellow Memorial Fund. He indicated he found the experience so disconcerting, "I wouldn't read in public again for $5,000 in cash or $1,000 worth of stock in The Century Company,"

Mrs. Aldrich in her book of reminiscences said the experience engendered "genuine stage fright," in her husband.

Rideing explained that Aldrich "warmed only to those who appealed to him through a kindred spirit. With others he could be cold and incommunicable enough."

While Rideing felt Aldrich "would have been at home in the age of Queen Anne (early 18th Century)," he also described him incredibly as "not illiberal," and considered him "a good bohemian" even in his Boston milieu. He once spotted Aldrich at Oscar's, a favorite Bean Town haunt, wearing "a flowing crimson scarf gathered at the neck by an antique ring," as an accent for "a quiet suit of tweeds."

Rideing's bohemian allusion contradicts Ferris Greenslet's biography written two years earlier.

"As time went on he cared less and less to revisit, even in memory, the glimpses of the bohemian . . . ," Greenslet maintained.

Paula Blanchard, in her biography of Sarah Orne Jewett, ascribed to Aldrich anti-social behavior in one regard:

"The xenophobia of Portsmouth native Thomas Bailey Aldrich...distrusted the railroad," she maintained despite the fact that his Uncle Charles Frost was a director of the Concord & Portsmouth Railroad company.

In a January 16, 1869 letter to the Rev. W. R. Alger, Aldrich notes that he made a donation of "a pair" of dollars for the welfare of one Henry Giles, who had experienced financial reversals and whose library had to be placed on the auction block. It seems likely that the small amount cited was a figurative one.

On Politics:

Volume 179 of "Contemporary Authors" describes his political view as "uninterested."

Alarmed by unlimited immigration, Aldrich became a lifetime member of the New England-based Immigration Restriction League, founded by Boston patricians at Harvard in 1894. Members included the then current president of Harvard, as well as Henry Cabot Lodge.

In a letter, Aldrich said that Bostonians were "full-blooded readers," while writers in New York had "no standing". He also said he was fortunate to have escaped Manhattan with his English intact. That is an interesting position in light of the fact that he spent a total of 18 years in New York City; from age four to age nine and from 16 to age 28.

According to Ferris Greenslet, his biographer, in a fit of hyperbole Aldrich boasted of having a coal bin inlaid with "mother-of-pearl and the skulls of tax-collectors."

"Personally, I believe that the possession of gold has ruined fewer men than lack of it," he wrote.

On Philip II of Spain: (reigned 1556-98):

"I hate nobody, living or dead, excepting Philip II of Spain [whose] one recorded hardy laugh was occasioned by the news of the St. Bartholomew Massacre,"[1] said Aldrich in "Ponkapog Papers." He described the king as the kind who could "mask his fanaticism or drop it for the time being when it seemed politic to do so." Aldrich dismissed England's Queen Mary (Bloody Mary), Philip's wife, from his unique hate list because he considered her "a maniac."

The occasion for his musings was an odd one. In his study, the maid while dusting had accidentally replaced an engraving of King Philip II on the mantel shelf upside down and Aldrich decided to leave it that way. If he loathed the king so much, why did he have the engraving in the first place?

Aldrich did not always leave the dusting to a maid. In a letter to his then landlord James Russell Lowell dated May 27, 1874, Aldrich claims to have "carefully dusted by my own hand" every volume in Lowell's library, prior to vacating the premises upon Lowell's return from Europe.

---

[1] In 1572, some 10,000 Huguenots were slaughtered in France by followers of Catherine de Medici, the queen mother. This became known as the St. Bartholomew's Day Massacre, to which Aldrich had referred.

On Originality:

The Merriam-Webster Dictionary of Quotations, July 1992 edition affords Aldrich the main entry in the subject category with his apt quatrain:

No bird has ever uttered note
That was not in some first bird's throat,
Since Eden's freshness and man's fall
No rose has been original.

X. TRAVELS

The year 1875 marked Aldrich's first European trip. He planned to leave in March and not return until January of the following year, spending extended periods in each country including England, France, Italy and Hungary. He left the six-year-old twins in the care of their grandmothers and "an aunt" according to Greenslet's biography. Aldrich was also known to have visited Spain and Scotland at least once and attended the decennial passion play at Oberammergau, Germany in 1890 and again in 1900. His known trips abroad include - but may not be limited to - Europe in 1875, 1879,1880, 1882, 1884, 1890, 1891, 1892 and 1900, and around the world in 1894-95 and 1898-99, as well as a summer trip in 1905 to Egypt, which included his son Talbot, who became engaged to a New England girl in their touring party, while in Cairo. Aldrich was also known to have been in Hong Kong, having written a letter to his sons from that locale on December 9, 1894.

In 1860, on his Uncle Charles Frost's yacht, Aldrich made a summer cruise from New York to Portsmouth to visit his grandparents.

In early 1875 the Aldriches boarded the S.S. Abyssinia for England and took an apartment at a London hotel, where Mrs. Aldrich in her memoirs made folly of Smith, a fortiesh manservant for dropping or adding inappropriately the letter "h" in his speech.

"Our summer abroad was without a flaw. I cannot say without a flea," declared Aldrich about that first trip aboard.

Aldrich had an audience with the head of the Catholic Church, Pope Pius IX (who, was subsequently designated a candidate for sainthood under Pope John Paul II). The pope, born, Giovanni M. Mastai Ferretti in Ancona, Italy, was 83 at the time.

Apparently, Aldrich sought the audience because it was the thing to do, certainly not because of any religious conviction. However, being an American of a Protestant faith, he found it unnerving when told he would have to kneel before the pontiff and that if one failed to do so, one would be ushered out of the room. He knelt.

Earlier he excoriated Mrs. Aldrich for making an unconscionably expensive purchase of amber rosary beads in a shop by the Spanish steps, paying what Aldrich claimed was close to three times the normal cost.[1]

Aldrich, who, in this memoir, refers to his wife only as "Madama," for some reason, noted that she did not have a wholly black dress, which was *de rigueur* for women in an audience before the pope. So Mrs. Aldrich took a Parisian black silk dress with turquoise-blue accents and had all the non-black color removed.

On January 8, 1879 once again aboard the Cunard steamer Abyssinia, Aldrich wrote on a scrap of paper he designated James M. Bugbee, a writer, to serve as guardian of the twins "in case anything should happen to us," One wonders if the seas were especially rough that day.

Aldrich, unlike Twain (with whom he was traveling on this European trip), was not given to swearing. However, in Paris, when Aldrich gave up his seat in a horse-drawn

---

[1] Although Aldrich describes them as "amber" the ones held by the museum appear to be of ebony according to Carolyn Roy formerly of the curatorial department. Taking Mrs. Aldrich's character into consideration, this writer believes it is possible her purchased beads may be the same rosary beads which originally rested in a showcase in the brick museum with a card directed by her to read: "Gift from Pope." Aldrich's narrative regarding the visit notes the pontiff did bless rosaries presented to his holiness, but makes no mention of any distribution of them as gifts.

car to a man who he thought was crippled and using a crutch, later realized it was a length of beaded walnut molding.

"Damn a dam'd man who would carry a dam'd piece of beading under his dam'd arm," he exclaimed.

Aldrich's son Talbot, then 13, wrote his parents in July of 1882 from Lynn, Massachusetts where his two grandmothers were taking care of him and his twin brother Charles while the Aldriches were vacationing with Henry Pierce, former mayor of Boston. Two such letters are on file in the Houghton Library at Harvard.

In the letter to his mother he sketches a penknife similar to the one Pierce had given him some time ago, but which he subsequently lost. "I want you to bring me home one like it," he demands.

In a subsequent one to his father whom he calls "Papa," he draws a steamboat to illustrate one near where he was staying.

"Horace [Wilson, a friend], Charlie and I want to get a steamboat next year very much indeed and Horace is going to work for his father this year in his office and Mr. Wilson said that all the money he earns he could put in a steamboat. Charles and I want to put some money with his so we can own some part of the boat with Horace," Talbot declared.

Whether the three boys achieved their goal is not known, but Talbot himself eventually owned a yacht, as did his father.

On July 24, 1884, in a letter to Horace Scudder, who filled in for him at The Atlantic Monthly during his extended European vacations (a duty Scudder came to resent), Aldrich, writing from London noted an outbreak of cholera had abbreviated his plans and he would board the ship "Alaska" on August 16 for home.

"My Russian plan died the day after our arrival in London," he wrote, "and the idea of Norway collapsed yesterday."

Aldrich explained that the northern European ports were under quarantine, "so our trip abroad has been sort of a failure."

When Mrs. Aldrich traveled abroad, she was accompanied by a maid, who at one point was listed simply as: "G. Symonds." According to Amelia Patch, who was with the Aldrich Museum for decades, James W. Hannon "had been butler for Thomas Bailey Aldrich for years . . . went 'round the world with him [and] was with him when he died."

During the summer of 1885, Aldrich went on a cruise on E. C. Benedict's yacht, Oneida with – among others - Laurence Hutton, author/critic and Edwin Booth, who, in a letter to his daughter wrote that "Aldrich is kept to a white heat of fun by Hutton."

In 1886 Aldrich found himself with Hutton on the same yacht in another cruise and in July, 1887 he cruised Maine waters with Booth. These references are found in the Hutton memoir and in the biography of Booth "Prince of Players."

In 1891 he toured Europe and the following year spent the entire summer there. According to Paulo Warth Gick, in his Aldrich thesis, he left his Boston home May 17, 1892 for his home in Ponkapog where he stayed until June 13, when he left for New York to embark two days later.

On March 31, 1893, he wrote Henry Lee Higginson of a recent return from New York to Boston where he was in the process of closing his affairs in preparation for an extended trip until October or November.

On October 14, 1894, while a guest at the Hotel Vancouver in Vancouver, British Columbia, Aldrich wrote his then 26-year-old son, Talbot, nicknamed Tal, a kind of chatty inconsequential letter.

In January 1896, the same year his friend Henry Pierce suffered what became a fatal stroke, the Aldriches went with him on a three-month cruise to Cuba and other parts of the West Indies on the latter's yacht "Hermione".

On August 23, 1898 he wrote his friend, Edmund C. Stedman that he planned to sail September 2, and remain abroad for a period of 10 months to a year!

December 24, 1898 found him at the Queens Hotel, in Kandy, Ceylon.

In January 1899 the Aldriches took a two-month Caribbean cruise in the company of Sarah Orne Jewett with stopovers at Nassau, the Bahamas; Port au Prince, Haiti and Jamaica. This was also on the "Hermione," presumably acquired following Pierce's death.

He wrote of setting sail on February 10, 1900 from New York to Spain on the Bismarck, planning to spend about eight months overseas. On April 15 he wrote Robert U. Johnson that he spent Holy Week in Rome, where he was still staying, which impressed his Unitarian sensibilities negatively.

"Holy Moses! What a week!," he wrote from the Grand Hotel D'Europe. "Candles, cardinals and cardinals! I've been to enough cathedrals to last me two life times. The more I see of these things the less devout I become. A year in Rome would turn me into an athesist [atheist]."

In April 29 in another letter to Johnson from Parker's Hotel, Lake Tramontano, Naples he said "I have been having a heavenly time all over Southern Italy. Now we are going to Venice and the Italian lakes."

In that earlier April 15 Johnson letter, he had said he planned to visit Constantinople, Turkey and Greece before doubling back to Paris in June. Those plans were changed in May by the illness of Mrs. Aldrich's sister, Martha, who had married William Streeter Richardson on February 20, 1890.

"The sister," he wrote Johnson on May 21 from Ponkapog, "is very very ill. We did not expect to find her alive. She has rallied, but I fear she will never leave her bed." According to the New England Historical and Genealogical Register, Mrs. Richardson did not succumb until more than two years later in November, 1902. The nature of her illness was not disclosed.

As for the Atlantic crossing, Aldrich said, "I have never made such an ideal voyage." He noted that the trip from Naples to New York had "simply entrancing moonlight nights" with a total of "thirteen days and nights of glossy sea."

In 1901 Aldrich was making plans to head south, though this writer was unable to uncover any more detail.

In 1905, Aldrich took a cruise along the coast aboard his son Talbot's yacht, "Bethulia."

He spent time in St. Augustine, Florida, and Jekyll Island, Georgia, owned by the exclusive J.I. Club.

On one trip on board a ship from Gibraltar to Morocco, he spotted a fez-crowned man dispensing, he said "thin sour wine from a goatskin, which he bore under his arm. I tested this wine and came to the conclusion that death by thirst was not without its advantages.

In Italy he concluded that "if an Italian shopkeeper should be submitted to a chemical analysis, and his rascality carefully separated from the other ingredients and thrown away, there would be nothing left of him."

On Tipping:

"...a man of ordinary agility might walk over the greater part of Europe on outstretched palms."

"I have paid a Neapolitan ten *sous* for leaning against a deadwall in front of a hotel window."

"The slightest thing will serve in Italy, for a lien upon your exchequer."

Aldrich mentions that an urchin who stands on his head expects a tip as well as girls throwing no fewer than 50 nosegays of dying flowers "showered upon you from Pompeii to Sorrento." He called the girls "little witches" and said they were "pretty enough to sculpt."

In another observation, he claimed an Irish

panhandler's brogue was so impossibly thick he could have employed it as a conveyance to cross the Atlantic.

"I informed him in English that I was a Frenchman and didn't understand him." Adding hyperbole to his mendacity, Aldrich concluded: "On the rising and falling inflection of that brogue I returned to America quite independent of a Cunard steamer. I had to call the man back and pay my passage."

Touring Tokio (the then current spelling) and Yokohama, he drank sake and said the food ranged from "tasting delicious" to tasting like "unpleasant drugs".

He was known to have toured the czarist empire in 1882, and on one trip, Aldrich spotted a youth reading "The Story of a Bad Boy."

XII. EARLY LOVES

Ferris Greenslet, in his Aldrich biography, disingenuously speaks of "affairs of young sentiment" in New York, in Portsmouth and in Boston.

Aldrich had just turned 19 when in a November 28, 1855 letter to his teenage friend, William Winter he writes of an inspiring rendezvous with a lady.

"Have I ever spoken to you of Miss Alice Cary? I spent last evening with her, and had a cozy talk about books – she and I alone. She is so beautiful and simple and good that I love her," Aldrich wrote. "She has written some beautiful poetry."

In all accuracy, this writer has not been able to determine whether Aldrich was truly romantically smitten or simply enthralled to be in the company of Miss Cary who was 16 years his senior.

At Idlewild, the Hudson River home of Nathanial Parker Willis, who had awarded Aldrich the assistant editorship of the Home Journal, Aldrich met Willis' daughter, Imogene, who had blue eyes and light brown hair, and was taken by her, according to Lilian Aldrich, writing in "Crowding Memories."

The summer before meeting Phoebe Garnant, a black-eyed beauty with French bloodlines, Aldrich went on a moonlight ride with a young friend of his mother and became engaged to her. Mrs. Aldrich in "Crowding Memories" does not mention her by name. Could she have been the same woman to whom Aldrich, while summering in Portsmouth alluded in a July, 1859 letter to R. H. Stoddard, the writer, when he wrote: "I'm in clover as you may imagine. To see her every day!"?

Aldrich met Phoebe Garnant (various references give other spellings to her last name, including Garnalt, Garnault and Garnutt) in Portsmouth, who was visiting his closest friend (name not listed by Lilian Aldrich in "Crowding Memories".) This writer's best guess is that the friend was Albert Laighton, the guileless poet.

Aldrich was so taken by her, he confessed as much to his then – unnamed - fiancée and left it to her to break the engagement. She did so by returning his ring and letters tied in a blue ribbon.

Aldrich became Miss Garnant's suitor. She was the ward of Wendell Phillips. In keeping with the times, Aldrich asked her guardian for permission to court her and it was granted. The spirited suitor failed to win her hand because of his indifference to abolition. Miss

Garnant, a decided abolitionist, rejected him on this basis after nearly a year's separation – a separation by her own request – during which time Aldrich wrote her diligently, several - one reference states four - letters each month.

Wendell Phillips was himself a radical abolitionist. Born in 1811, he served as president of the American Anti-Slavery Society, from 1865-79, and was a pro-immigration activist and an advocate of women's rights. Years after the ill-fated courtship of his ward, Phillips wrote Aldrich on October 20, 1881, thanking him for his condolences over the loss of a loved one. Although virtually everything Phillips was for, Aldrich was against - or at best indifferent - after the abolitionist died in 1884, Aldrich wrote a poem titled: "Monody, on the Death of Wendell Phillips," the last line of which implores: "God send his like again."

He was urged to incorporate in his editorial columns pro-abolition themes, detailing measures for eliminating slavery, but Aldrich chose not to do so.

Miss Garnant later married George W. Smalley, who established the London bureau of the same New York Tribune for which Aldrich had worked in 1861. She had lived in the Phillips household for 11 years until her marriage. One reference states that they married in 1860, another 1862, another 1863 and still another January 18,

1864[1]. Yet another reference has her entering Aldrich's own life in 1862.

Greenslet, in his biography, speaks of Aldrich's "youthful affair of the heart, which in this [1861] summer ended, as a first love should, unhappily." Whether he was referring to Phoebe Garnant, or the young otherwise unidentified woman whom he had break off their engagement in order to court Miss Garnant is unknown. In either case, she would not have been his "first love" since his infatuation with Imogene Willis presumably holds that distinction.

In 1875 Phoebe, as Mrs. Smalley, invited the Aldriches to her and her husband's home in London. Among other distinguished invited dinner guests was Robert Browning, the poet and playwright. Overcome with emotion at seeing the early love of his life, Aldrich pressed his wife's hand when she asked "How lovely she is, how can you bear it?" He replied "by grinding my teeth

[1] The latter date is attributed to the Atlanta Journal, admittedly an odd source in view of the raging Civil War. The newspaper apparently took the time and space to report the nuptials as having taken place in Boston, Massachusetts. Despite the bitter rivalry, the Union and Confederacy allowed a free exchange of newspapers. The wedding was apparently newsworthy on the basis of Smalley's war correspondent record.

and thinking of the twins." This astounding quote appears in Mrs. Aldrich's own memoirs.

Whatever qualms Mrs. Aldrich might have felt in encountering her husband's early infatuation it was subsumed in favor of Mr. Smalley's reputation and connections.

"It was not entirely as a newspaper correspondent that Mr. Smalley gained his reputation," Mrs. Aldrich wrote in her memoir. "He was a critic in art, music and the drama; he had the *entrée* of the highest circles of the social life of England, was the confidant of [William Ewart] Gladstone[1] and the intimate of many prominent men on the Continent."

It is tempting to conjecture her social-climbing aspirations may have been the inspiration for Sinclair Lewis' spoiled matron in "Dodsworth" published in 1929, just two years after Mrs. Aldrich's death.

When Aldrich and Phoebe Garnant parted ways, he said he could still render affection to another but <u>never</u> love. Incredibly, this sentiment was recorded in Mrs. Aldrich's memoir. It is even more amazing that the Houghton Library at Harvard University houses letters written between the Aldriches and the Smalleys from at

[1] British prime minister

least 1886 to 1897 (a year before the Smalleys separated) and that Mrs. Smalley continued to correspond with Mrs. Aldrich after the latter's husband died, from 1913 to 1920.

In those archives is a letter dated October 20, 1886 from Smalley himself writing from New York: "delighted to be your guest" presumably in response to an Aldrich invitation.

In 1897, the year before the Smalleys divorce was finalized, Mrs. Smalley, listed in the Social Register as living at 20 East 75th Street, New York City, had her children Phillips, Emerson, Eleanor, Evelyn and Ida with her. Phillips Smalley (1875-1939), named after Mrs. Smalley's childhood guardian Wendell Phillips, worked as a silent film director from 1911-19 and thereafter as an actor until his death.

At the time of Aldrich's death, Mrs. Smalley was living at 328 West 57th Street, New York and sent Mrs. Aldrich a letter of condolence now on file at the Houghton Library, Harvard.

"My dear friend," she wrote. "Ever since Mrs. [William Dean] Howells told me of your dear husband's illness, my heart and thoughts have been with you both, and I longed to write and tell you so, and how no words will come to help me express to you my deepest sympathy in this terrible sorrow. No one is all the world can know better than I what this loss means to you, and I feel as if the last link that bound me to the happiest days of my youth had broken. Do accept the most heartfelt sympathy of Evelyn [Phoebe's daughter] and your old friend."

On December 20, 1920 from that same address, she wrote Mrs. Aldrich at her Ponkapog home, possibly for the last time. On file at the Houghton Library at Harvard, it reads:

"Dear Silent-Lady, I wrote you a long (for me) letter of thanks & appreciation the very day (long ago) after receiving your delightful book ["Crowding Memories" no doubt] – and letting you know of dear [daughter] Evelyn's return from the wars & her plan to go to Boston for a few day as she still hopes to do - & I want her to see you and you to see her. Her experiences are unusual. I write that dear thing as I have not heard a word from you and fear you may not have received my letter which I sent to Ponkapog. Should you not have done so you will think my silence very strange. As I write with difficulty – I send only these few words to take your love and the dear memory of other days. Evelyn sails for France to renew her work, just after Xmas – with happy wishes for you all. Affectionately, Phoebe."

XIII. MRS. ALDRICH

Mary Elizabeth Woodman who married Thomas Bailey Aldrich while he was on the rebound from a failed courtship with Phoebe Garnant, outlived her husband by 20 years. In those two decades she seemed determined to create the myth that "The Story of a Bad Boy," was in fact her husband's life story as an adolescent. As a result this myth continues to have worldwide implications. Even his contemporaries mix the facts of his life with the fiction of the book. A plaque in the city-owned Thomas Bailey Aldrich memorial park has three errors in fact. It states he inherited his maternal grandfather's house – he never did. It cites his arrival from New Orleans to live with his grandparents as 1846 – it was 1849. Most damming of all – and this is attributed to Mrs. Aldrich's campaign – it cites his grandfather's last name as Nutter from the novel when it was Bailey.

This writer believes her motives were manifold. Cognizant of the hundreds of queries to her husband as to whether or not the children's book was authentic she simply confirmed what questioners wanted to believe as totally true story. She established the museum complex filled with furnishings that may or may not have been there during her husband's boyhood residency. Equally important was Mrs. Aldrich's apparent determination to perpetuate its publication; edition after edition. The result is that it is still in print today as it has been since 1869.

Following her husband's death, Mrs. Aldrich was known to have written scores of letters to Houghton Mifflin, his - and eventually her - publisher over the next 20 years until her demise. This writer has been unable to unearth them; presumably, they pertain to royalties, contracts and related subjects, though she may have retained an attorney to handle those matters. It is not beyond the realm of possibility however, knowing her demeanor, that some of the letters may have been critical in nature.

On her first meeting with Samuel Clemens/Mark Twain, (possibly the winter of 1871-72, though "Selected Mark Twain-Howells Letters" lists 1868 as their first encounter, unlikely since the Twain-to-Aldrich letter of January 15, 1871 suggests **no** prior relationship), he had been ushered into her home by her husband, who, in an inexplicable breach of etiquette simply said to Twain: "my wife" but failed to introduce him to Mrs. Aldrich. Another version has him mumbling Twain's name so his wife was unable to discern it.

Having recently experienced another unexpected guest for whom she had to stretch dinner for two into dinner for three, she alerted a servant not to announce dinner on this latest occasion. In the earlier experience, Mrs. Aldrich found her husband devouring too many oysters and sweetmeats and kept kicking him under the table to desist so that the unexpected guest might have his share. Afterward while presumably preparing for bed, Mrs. Aldrich asked her husband why he had not heeded her non-verbal admonitions only to be told he felt nothing. It turned out that she had been kicking the guest! No wonder - she reasoned with horror - the guest kept looking at her in an alarming manner.

With this new guest (Twain) she found him contrarily dressed, wearing summer and winter clothing; with a gray winter sealskin coat and hat turned fur-side out (and therefore wrong-side for the style of the day), yellowish-brown summer trousers, a violet bow tie, and low black shoes instead of presumably taller, more stylish footwear. He walked with a lolling gait, which was his style, but Mrs. Aldrich, not knowing his style, interpreted it as a drunken pace, when coupled with his "odd manner of speaking" (which no doubt would be attributable to his Missouri drawl).

Time went on, the quarter-hour, the half-hour, etc. and finally Twain, with a harrumph no doubt, excused himself and left the Aldrich house.

Aldrich turned to his wife, perplexed and angry and asked why she had not invited Twain to dinner. When she realized who he was (apparently, Aldrich assumed she knew him from photographs; or it may have been a puerile prank) she wailed and attempted to have her husband summon Twain back. Alas Aldrich did not and Mrs. Aldrich said it was many years before the incident was explained fully to Twain. The damage however appeared to be permanent.

Twain's strong personality occasionally clashed with others. William Dean Howells, the editor of The Atlantic Monthly, was miffed when Twain had his nephew, instead of himself, write.

"If Mr. Clemens is disabled or in trouble, or has some unknown offence [sic] with me, I can understand his preferring to write to his friend by the hand of his agent," Howells responded.

In another incident Howells declined an invitation from the Aldriches, giving as his reason that he did not wish to come when Twain was there "and play second fiddle to him." These two episodes are revealed in Edward Wagenknecht's 1969 biography of Howells.

Twain was not unaware of his contrary nature. In an encounter with Laurence Hutton, the actor Otis Skinner noted Hutton's receipt of a Twain letter in which he supposedly had delivered his farewell lecture, only to succumb to still another personal appearance.

"In short," Twain wrote, "there is nothing that prevents my becoming a harlot but my sex."

One of Mrs. Aldrich's most incredible relationships as related by Samuel Clemens/Mark Twain in his autobiography is with Charles Frederick Worth, the epitome of *haute couture*. Born in England in 1825, Worth achieved international success through his salon in Paris and designs for French Empress Eugénie and other royalty. His creations undoubtedly commanded hundreds of dollars and defined his reputation and he naturally insisted on a number of fittings with a client before the sale was fully executed. **That** stipulation strange to say, Mrs. Aldrich refused to accept. According to Twain she threw a tantrum, declaring that she would not abide multiple fittings and vowed not to do business with his salon ever again!

Interpreting her origins, Twain asserted that Mrs. Aldrich "had been a pauper all her life" but he also demurred by acknowledging: "For the protection of the reader I must confess that I am perhaps prejudiced."

This writer has not been able to verify Mrs. Aldrich's background in terms of her parents' financial viability. As noted elsewhere in this book even where they were born is subject to variance.

Regarding Bret Harte, the western saga writer, who was professor of modern literature at the University of California in 1871 before moving to New York a few months later, Mrs. Aldrich wrote: "notwithstanding his Hebrew blood, he was born a spendthrift."

Harte, whose name at birth was Francis Brett Harte had a paternal grandfather Bernard, a devout Jew deeply involved with New York's first synagogue, Shearith Israel. His marriage to his first wife, Catharine Brett, a Gentile, had been kept secret and was not generally known. Their son Henry was Harte's father[1].

Her Literary Efforts

Mrs. Aldrich compiled a list of flowers mentioned by her late husband in his published works. "The Shadow of the Flowers," which includes a selection of his botanical

---

1 This information culled from several sources, including the Encyclopedia Judaica, via the Internet

references, was liberally illustrated by Talbot Aldrich, their son, and Carl J. Nordell in 1912. The Thomas Bailey Aldrich Memorial Association members deviated from these sources when it did the actual plantings. According to Anne Duncan, former landscape department head, Aldrich writes of some varieties native to Columbia, South America, which would not have thrived in New Hampshire gardens, so they were not planted.

The association purchased an additional lot, and in 1914 (another reference states 1920) planted hemlock trees among which a contemplative grove was created. The estate is composed of six parcels.

Mrs. Garland Patch, wife of the caretaker of the Aldrich Museum dedicated in 1908, refers to petunia and cherry, pear, plum and elm trees, as well as gooseberry bushes on the grounds. When dedicated, the garden had raised beds and geometric cobblestone walkways. The very next year the walkways were replaced by patterns of brick.

There is also inconsistency in just what was where. Originally, in the yard there were two elm trees and a quarter-acre of purple plum trees and gooseberry bushes. The elms were removed by the original museum association and the plum trees and gooseberry bushes not replaced to date.

Also, in his so-called *roman à clef*, when Aldrich sneaks out of the house for the Fourth of July bonfire, he falls into rose bushes in front of the house. However, a lack of space precludes flora of any size at the main entrance. Additionally, the description of the house is that it was set back from Court Street. That certainly is not the case now in terms of configuration of the street and sidewalk. Another inconsistency is that Aldrich, in "The Story of a Bad Boy" implies the long case or pendulum clock (later known as a grandfather clock) is by the front door. Postcards printed when the museum first opened show the clock by the back door. Perhaps as a boy, Aldrich considered the back door his "front" door, since he may have used it more often.

Some of the references noted in "The Shadow of the Flowers," include hyacinth and goldenrod in his poem, "Elmwood;" violets and cowslip in "Spring in New England;" snowdrops, pansies, heather in "Flower and Thorn;" and white lily in "A Child's Grave."

John Forti the museum's former curator of historic landscape had found reference to lilacs growing in the back yard:

"I am glad to come to Portsmouth when they were purpling, for they bloomed here in Thomas Bailey

Aldrich's boyhood; they perfumed the pages of his books," wrote Alice Van Leer Carrick about the Aldrich Museum in 1919.

In 1925, two years before she died Mrs. Aldrich had published "Choice Receipts," dedicated to a Major Dobbin. Oddly she chose to write her preface in the third person singular.

"When she began making these memoranda, it was with no view of serving any one except herself; but the constant applications she has had for copies of this or that receipt have suggested to her the expediency of printing them," states Mrs. Aldrich, employing the older word "receipt" for the more popular one "recipe".

Some of the recipes are so simple as to border on the inane. An example is for orange marmalade toast: "Thin slices of bread toasted on one side. Butter the other side and spread generously with orange marmalade and toast this side. Serve at once." Others such as Christmas cake called for a baker's dozen of ingredients. More helpful perhaps, are hints on how to keep an ice chest free of bacterial growth; to cleanse coffee pots with boiled wood ashes and to sprinkle salt on a rug when sweeping it.

"It prevents dust rising and brightens the colors," Mrs. Aldrich wrote, explaining this last tip.

XIV. LAST DAYS

"Longfellow," a poem written for the centenary of Henry Wadsworth Longfellow's 1807 birth (he died in 1882), was completed only a short time before Aldrich's death. He had once hoped to be taught by Longfellow, a professor at Harvard, but he never matriculated, though corresponded with him for decades and dined with him in his -Aldrich's- Boston home.

Aldrich died at his home in Beacon Hill, Boston, on March 19, 1907 at 5:30 p.m., following an operation. As he was Unitarian, church services were conducted at the Arlington Street Church in Boston, built in 1729 originally for a different Protestant denomination than the Unitarian[1] designation it was operating under at the time of Aldrich's death. The church has been operating as a Unitarian Universalist institution, at least since World War II. Aldrich is buried in Mt. Auburn Cemetery, Cambridge, Massachusetts, next to his son, Charles.

---

[1] Unitarianism is an outgrowth of New England Congregationalism that began in the third quarter of the 1700s.

Aldrich was fatalistic about his illness.

Prior to his death, he had developed an internal infection and, according to the Portsmouth Herald, had a premonition about his demise.

He had fallen ill on January 31, 1907, and was taken to the Homeopathic Hospital on East Concord Street, Boston. The operation was apparently successful, but Aldrich died presumably of complications following a relapse. He had been taken from the hospital to his home on March 17, upon his own request.

Aldrich said to a friend at about that time: "For myself, I regard death merely as the passing shadow on a flower."

With his last look and smile he said: "In spite of all, I am going to sleep; put out the lights."

Upon Aldrich's death, his surviving twin son, Talbot, who kept homes at 80 Mount Vernon Street in Boston and Tenants Harbor, Maine, was quoted in a Portsmouth newspaper: "I have heard him termed time and again that eternal boy."

In a January 27, 1903 letter to Charles E. Norton, co-founder of The Nation, Aldrich had expressed gratitude for the return of letters he had written to James Russell Lowell years ago, and waxed nostalgic:

"One or two of them seemed like ghosts come to tell me how very young I once was. Yet I would be willing today to have as little sense, if I could have as much youth as I had when I penned those faded pages," he mused.

As for both his parents, Talbot said: "My mother and he have always been like a pair of young lovers." He said they had been apart just two weeks in 42 years of marriage "and I have heard him say: 'two weeks too many'."

Once, in declining a Fourth of July rendezvous Aldrich wrote his prospective host: "Mrs. Aldrich has made an arrangement for herself, and I never celebrate anything without her."

Talbot's grandson, Jonathan Aldrich, disclosed at the October 5, 2002 memorial service for his father Bailey Aldrich, in the Memorial Church, at Harvard Yard, that he too is a writer of poetry. Describing some recent works as "a series of fairy tale-sounding poems," he disclosed his father's fondness for one titled "The Father," elements of which might well evoke the work of his great-grandfather, Thomas Bailey Aldrich.

It reads in part:

Let me take you by the hand, old gentleman.
There may be a few stories we haven't told
each other and the hour is growing late

Apparently neither Jonathan Aldrich's illustrious ancestor nor the latter's wife enjoyed the best of health throughout their more than four decades of marriage. Letters from Sarah Orne Jewett (1849-1909), which her intimate friend Annie Fields (1834-1915) had published posthumously, suggest as much.

Writing to the Aldriches circa 1889, she states: "I hope that there may be a little better news from you two old invalids – that these are days of less pain and discomfort." That same year, Charles Warren (1846-1924) held Aldrich's power of attorney, according to a letter on file in the Houghton Library at Harvard.

In a letter to Mrs. Aldrich dated November, 1891, Miss Jewett, writing from her home in South Berwick, Maine, states: "I was so grieved to hear of your illness," noting that she was distressed to hear "that you are not quite well yet."

Most of the above information on Aldrich's death – except where noted - comes from the newspaper archives in the Portsmouth Public Library.

Mark Twain said: "The country has lost a most exquisite artist in verse."

"The well poised mind and deliberate art always characteristic of Aldrich seemed to imply reserved power," wrote Henry C. Vedder, one of his biographers, "but the crowning masterpiece never came."

"The place of Aldrich in American Literature will be determined by posterity," declared William Winter, his literary colleague and virtual life-long friend.

The Widow Aldrich wasted no time in settling her late husband's affairs. According to Marshall S. Berdan, three weeks after his burial she sold The Porcupine, his impressive country house in Saranac Lake. Their Ponkapog estate, the Redman Farm, said by Howard S. Whitley, an attorney to have been tenured by Henry Pierce as a "life interest" to the couple, became part of the Hills Reservation.

She also took to traveling. There is a dispatch that – sometime prior to her death in 1927 – she sailed for Europe and then took an automobile tour through Wales and Scotland before stopping over in London and planning other tourist trips.

Talbot, who had relocated from 80 Mount Vernon St. to 34 Fairfield St. about 1910, moved with his wife Eleanor to his parents' fashionable Beacon Hill home following his mother's death.

In a posthumous honor the United States of America, on June 8, 1942 launched the Liberty ship, the USS Thomas Bailey Aldrich at Portland, Oregon.

For his own legacy, Aldrich wrote Robert U. Johnson,

associate editor of The Century Magazine, these words when reaching a dry period in his creativity:

"If I have written anything my countrymen care to keep, I have written enough; if I have written nothing worth keeping, I have written too much."

Mark M.A. DeWolfe Howe in his 1922 book "Memories of a Hostess: a Chronicle of Eminent Friendships Drawn Chiefly from the Diaries of Mrs. James T. Fields," widow of one of Aldrich's predecessors on the Atlantic Monthly, printed some musings she penned during a cruise:

"[Aldrich] is a worshipper of the English language . . . so natural, finding fault at times, without being a fault-finder, and being crusty like another human creature when out of sorts – but on the whole a most refreshing companion, coming up from below [deck] every morning with a shining countenance, his hair curling like a boy's and ready for a new day. He said yesterday that he should like to live 450 years."

Mrs. Fields noted Aldrich had alluded to *déjà vu* and

reincarnation in specific detail.

His near life-long friend, William Winter, writing in his 1909 memoir about Aldrich and his contemporaries summed up this fact of life so well:

"It is a fact within the experience of every close observer of his time that men and women of extraordinary ability and charm pass across the scene and vanish from it, leaving a potent impression of character, of mind, and even of genius, yet leaving no endurable evidence of their exceptional worth. Such persons, of whom the world hears nothing, are, sometimes, more interesting than some persons – writers and the like – of whom the world hears much. They deserve commemoration; occasionally they receive it."

This writer holds the hope that readers of this book have found this to be one of those occasions.

BIBLIOGRAPHY

Aldrich, J. James, "George Aldrich Genealogy, Descendants of George Aldrich of Mendon, Massachusetts," vol. 1, Service Press & Lithography Co., 1971.

Aldrich, Thomas Bailey, "The Story of a Bad Boy," originally 1869, University Press of New England, 1990 reprint.

__ "From Ponkapog to Pesth," Houghton Mifflin, 1883.

__ "Ponkapog Papers," Houghton Mifflin, 1903.

Aldrich, Mrs. Thomas Bailey, "The Shadow of the Flowers," Houghton Mifflin, 1912.

__ "Crowding Memories," Houghton Mifflin, 1920.

__ "Choice Receipts," Houghton Mifflin, the Riverside Press, 1925.

Beer, Thomas, "The Mauve Decade, American Life at the End of the Nineteenth Century," Alfred A. Knopf, 1926.

Belford, Barbara, "Oscar Wilde, a Certain Genius," Random House, 2000.

Blanchard, Paula, "Sarah Orne Jewett," Addison-

Wesley Publishing Co., 1994.

Bolton, Sarah K., "Famous American Authors," Thomas Y. Cromwell & Co., 1887.

Brighton, Raymond A., "They Came to Fish," Peter E. Randall, publisher, 1979.

Duryee, Samuel S., Jr., "The Life of Thomas Bailey Aldrich," Newcomen Publications, Princeton University Press, 1951.

Ellman, Richard, "Oscar Wilde," Alfred A. Knopf, 1988.

Fields, Annie "Letters of Sarah Orne Jewett," Houghlin Mifflin, 1911.

Frost, John Eldridge, "Sarah Orne Jewett," Cabinet Press, 1960.

Greenslet, Ferris, "Thomas Bailey Aldrich," Houghton Mifflin, 1908.

Gurney, C.S. "Portsmouth Historic and Picturesque," Strawbery Banke, Peter E. Randall, publisher, 1981 edition.

Howe, Mark M. A. DeWolfe, "Memories of a Hostess: a Chronicle of Eminent Friendships Drawn Chiefly from the Diaries of Ms. James T. Fields, Atlantic Monthly, 1922.

Howells,W.D. "My Mark Twain" Harper & Brothers, 1910.

Jacobson, Marcia, 'Being a Boy Again – Autobiography and the American Boy Books," University of Alabama Press, 1994.

Kaplan, Justin "Mr. Clemens and Mr. Twain," Touchstone, 1966.

Korngold, Ralph, "Two Friends of Man," Little, Brown. 1950

Little, Nina Fletcher, "Little by Little," E.P. Dutton, Inc., 1984.

Matthiesson, Francis Otto, "Sarah Orne Jewett," Houghton Mifflin, 1929.

Moore, Isabel, "Talks in a Library with Laurence Hutton," C.P. Putnam's Sons, the Knickerbocker Press, 1905.

Paine, Albert Bigelow, "Mark Twain a Biography," Harper & Brothers, 1912.

Rideing, William H., "Glimpses of T.B. Aldrich," Putnam's Magazine, vol. 7, 1910.

Ruggles, P. Eleanor, "Prince of Players," W.W. Norton & Co., 1953.

Samuels, Charles E., "Thomas Bailey Aldrich," Twayne Publishers, 1965.

Scudder, Horace Elisha, "James Russell Lowell," vol. 2, Houghton, Mifflin, 1901.

Sedgwick, Ellery, "The Atlantic Monthly," University

of Massachusetts Press, 1994.

"Selected Mark Twain-Howells Letters 1872-1910," the Belknap Press of Harvard University Press, 1967.

Silverstone, Elizabeth, "Sarah Orne Jewett, a Writer's Life," Overlook Press, 1993.

Skinner, Cornelia Otis, "Family Circle," Houghton Mifflin, 1948.

Steusbaugh, John, "History of Greenwich Village," Harper Colllins, 2013

Thaxter, Rosamond, "Sandpiper, the Life and Letters of Celia Thaxter," Peter E. Randall, publisher, fourth printing, 1982.

Ticknor, Caroline, "Glimpses of Authors," Houghton Mifflin, 1922.

Twain, Mark "The Autobiography of Mark Twain," Harper, 1959.

Twain, Mark, "Mark Twain in Eruption," Harper & Brothers, 1940.

Vedder, Henry C., "American Writers of Today," Silver, Burdett & Co., 1894 and 1910.

Wallace, Irving, "The Fabulous Showman – The Life and Times of P.T. Barnum," Alfred A. Knopf, 1959.

Wagenknecht, Edward, 'William Dean Howells, the Friendly Eye," Oxford University Press, 1969.

Whittaker, Robert H., "Land of Lost Content: the

Piscataway River Basin and the Isles of Shoals: the People, their Dreams, their History," Alan Sutton, publisher, 1993.

Winter, William "Old Friends, Being Literary Recollections of Other Days," Books for Library Press, 1971 reprint.

OTHER SOURCES

Berdan, Marshall S., "The Hollow Days," Adirondack Life Online, December 2002.

Cosgrave, Mary Silva, the published lecture series on Thomas Bailey Aldrich, Horn Book Magazine, 1965.

Hazlett, C.A., "Reminiscences of Portsmouth Authors," The Granite Monthly, March 1915 issue.

"Dictionary of American Biography."

Donahue, Marie, written transcription of her lecture on Thomas Bailey Aldrich and his Seacoast circle, presented at St. John's Church, June 23, 1983.

Durel, John W., "From Strawbery Banke to Puddle Dock: the Evaluation of a Neighborhood, 1630-1850," in partial fulfillment of a University of New Hampshire doctorate degree, May 1984.

Houghton Library, Harvard University, listing of correspondence from and to Aldrich et. al.

Gick, Paulo Warth, "An Annotated Critical Edition of Unpublished Letters by Thomas Bailey Aldrich," thesis for the English Department Graduate School at Pennsylvania State University, 1982.

Nightingale, Amy, a Strawbery Banke research project, 1984.

"Periodical Literature in Nineteenth Century America," edited by Kenneth M. Price and Susan Belasco Smith, University of Virginia Press, 1995.

Pomerance, Benjamin, "Home Sweet Home" article on The Porcupine, Saranac Lake, N.Y.

Portsmouth City Directories, Portsmouth Chronicle, Portsmouth Herald, Portsmouth Journal, Springfield (Massachusetts) Republican, Boston-Transcript various dates. various encyclopedia, online sources and the Strawbery Banke Museum old house book to the Thomas Bailey Aldrich Museum.

Whitley, Howard S., " History of Ponkapoag Camp," as downloaded from internet June 2, 2013.